Also by John Hammond Moore –

*Before and After; or, The Relations of the Races at the South*

*Research Materials in South Carolina: A Guide*

*The American Alliance: Australia, New Zealand, and the United States, 1940-1970*

*The Juhl Letters to the Charleston Courier: A View of the South, 1865-1871*

*Albemarle: Jefferson's County, 1727-1976*

*Australians in America, 1876-1976*

*The Faustball Tunnel: German POWs in America and Their Great Escape*

*Over-Sexed, Over-Paid, and Over Here: Americans in Australia, 1941-1945*

*Wiley: One Hundred and Seventy-Five Years of Publishing*

*The South Carolina Highway Department, 1917-1987*

*South Carolina Newspapers*

*South Carolina in the 1880s: A Gazetter*

*Columbia and Richland County: A South Carolina Community, 1740-1990*

*A Plantation Mistress on the Eve of the Civil War*

*The Baileys of Clinton: A South Carolina Family*

*The Confederate Housewife*

*Southern Homefront*

*Wacko War: Strange Tales from America, 1941-1945*

*Carnival of Blood: Dueling, Lynching, and Murder in South Carolina, 1880-1920*

*The Voice of Small-Town America: The Selected Writings of Robert Quillen, 1920-1948*

## THE YOUNG ERROL
### Flynn before Hollywood

A fascinating account of the early life of one of Australia's most colourful and controversial sons. John Hammond Moore traces film star Errol Flynn's turbulent career from his birth in sedate Hobart through his eccentric schooldays and his youth in Sydney and cruising the Pacific to his years as a pioneer tobacco planter in Papua and the 'discovery' that led to Hollywood and stardom.

The author comments: 'While his golden age in Hollywood produced some wondrous swashbuckling, Errol Flynn was not really acting at all. He was merely transferring a natural style developed in Sydney, Port Moresby, Rabaul, and London to a much larger audience.'

Anecdotes, quotations from Flynn's own diaries and from people who knew him in Australia and Papua New Guinea crowd one upon the other to underscore this truth, and to embellish this rollicking tale of a man who in the author's words: 'lived for half a century the sort of life adolescents dream of but men dare not attempt.'

John Hammond Moore was born in Maine, U.S.A. in 1924. He attended Hamilton College and the University of Virginia and has worked as a journalist, editor and university lecturer in Australia and America. His published works include some fifty articles in historical and popular journals in both countries.

He lived in Australia from 1969 until 1971, and became interested in the life of Errol Flynn during a visit to Papua New Guinea for a professional conference in 1970.

# THE
# YOUNG ERROL

## Flynn Before
## Hollywood

## John Hammond Moore

www.trafford.com

North America & International
toll-free: 1 888 232 4444 (USA & Canada)
phone: 250 383 6864 ♦ fax: 812 355 4082

For Harry Paget Flashman, George MacDonald Fraser, and millions throughout the world who found the depression and war (warm, hot, cold, etc.) a bit more palatable thanks to the exploits on and off the screen of a Tasmanian lad grown to manhood –

ERROL LESLIE THOMSON FLYNN,
1909-1959

# Contents

In am going to front the essentials of life to see if I can learn what it has to teach and above all not to discover, when I come to die, that I have not lived.

I am going to live deeply, to acknowledge not one of these so-called forces which hold our lives in thrall & reduce us to economic dependency.

I am going to live sturdily & Spartan-like, to drive life into a corner & reduce it to its lowest terms mean then I'll know its meanness, and if I find it sublime I shall know it by experience—and not make wistful conjectures about it conjured up by illustrated magazines.

Lines from Errol Flynn's New Guinea<br>notebook (1933).

# Introduction

Dedication of these pages to Harry Flashmen should not be taken lightly. Readers who have rollicked their way through the first two volume of his papers cannot fail to discern therein some elements of a nineteenth century Errol. In fact, George MacDonald Fraser, editor and compiler of the Flashman saga, has inscribed *Royal Flash* (London, 1971) to, among others; the great Flynn himself. However, superficial comparison of Harry and Errol may be somewhat unfair. Volume one proclaims Flashman to be bully, liar, womanizer, coward... yet irresistible. Errol Flynn was, to some extent, all of these – but there was an essential difference. He assumed each role with much more style, grace, and charm than Harry Flashman could muster even in his balmiest days.

If bully, it was often to protect a weaker individual from yet another bully. If lying, he wove such gossamer tales that no one cared a whit whether they were listening to truth or fiction. Womanizer? Most assuredly so. A reporter who spent several hours with Flynn a year or so before his death recalls consummate charm, ribald remarks, and tantalizing tales *until* a good-looking specimen of the opposite sex entered the room. Then, he noted, "I might as well have not existed!"

Was Flynn, like Flashman, a coward? Probably not, although some New Guinea acquaintances of the late 1920s and early 1930s might disagree. Irresistible? Most certainly. Ken Hunter-Kerr, a Sydney friend, recalls walking through that city's King's Cross section with twenty-year-old Flynn was an "almost embarrassing" experience. Women of all ages, all shapes and sizes, made no secret of their eye-bulging admiration for his slim, six-foot-two, 170-pound form.

Yet, merely measuring Errol against Harry is not enough. For, as nearly as anyone can tell there was only one side to Harry the Flash—the callous, flesh-hungry scamp who romped from mattress to mattress. While this also may describe Errol to some blindly biased souls, there was certainly another Flynn. That Flynn was an urbane raconteur, aware of the most intricate and subtle niceties of drawing room etiquette. He was a superb athlete who proved his superiority on tennis court, football oval, and dance floor . . . and in the boxing ring as well. Despite an inclination to be lazy and a general disdain for mental exertion, he became a better than average writer and a shrewd manipulator of cards, be it poker, bridge, or what-have-you.

Flynn was, in short, a well-bred individual versed in the ways of gentlemen; yet, not far below that smooth exterior lurked the imp who could drop ice cream on the heads of august school masters, trade blows with the boys at the corner pub, or lure a healthy maid onto a coal pile for a lumpy experiment in teenage sex play. Perhaps herein lies the charm and attraction of Errol Flynn, whether on or off the screen. Unpredictable, witty, contemptuous of authority, apparently a rousing success as a male animal, he lived for half a century the sort of life adolescents dream of but men dare not attempt.

Unless one is a complete square, it is most difficult to dislike Errol Flynn. Let's say, for example, that you think him an unprincipled, sex-crazed rascal. Perhaps he was. But who among us has not dreamed of making a school teacher look foolish. . .of getting into the pants of a robust lovely. . .or crossing blades with the evil duke on the steps of the castle and winning the alabaster hand of Maid Marian. . . ?

Liar! Be quiet.

In August 1970, while trying to teach American history at a university in Sydney's sprawling suburbs, I attended a professional conference at Port Moresby in Papua and subsequently took a short tour of the New Guinea highlands to the north. Even before I left the Moresby area I began to hear bits of Flynniana. The pattern was always the same—at the Rouna Falls pub near Errol's old tobacco fields, in Wau where he worked as an air cargo clerk, at Lae where he delivered labor recruited from the surrounding hill country, and so on. Flynn departed in 1933 owing much money. When he became a famous Hollywood star his old pals wrote seeking payment, but instead each received a glossy autographed photo from the publicity boys at Warner Brothers. Apparently even a dentist-uncle in Sydney got similar satisfaction (or dissatisfaction). At least Errol was consistent and did not show partiality. In the tropics one is usually told that the photo was nailed to the privy door (or some spot within) where weather, insects, etc. made quick work of the star's proud features. What uncle did with his copy, I know not.

My favorite of these tales, and only a slight variation of the familiar theme, involves a New Guinea dentist named Eric Weine. A huge man, Weine once fought with Flynn in a pub fracas and, some years after Errol departed, had an ear bitten off during another brawl with a man named Sanderson. When one of Flynn's earliest Hollywood swashbucklers came to the islands, the whole town packed Jim Hoile's little movie hall at Salamaua. The film was greeted with a rousing chorus of "What about the money you owe me, Flynny?" Then, as cast listings and various credits trailed off (costumes and hair styles by so-and-so), a huge roar shook the entire building: ". . .AND TEETH BY ERIC WEINE ! ! ! "

Weine later commented that, when dealing with a bloody, son-of-a-bitch like Flynn, a dentist should use temporary fillings. Errol, by the way, was not the only customer to feel Big Eric's wrath. Weine once met a long overdue account in a pub and bluntly demanded to know when he might expect payment for a set of false teeth. The owner replied that actually the teeth were unsatisfactory and didn't fit well. Weine said he was mighty sorry to hear that . . . could he look at them and see what was wrong? The choppers were extracted, the burly dentist examined them closely, then dropped the teeth on the barroom floor, smashing them to bits with his heel. "No worries now, mate", said Weine. "Account's closed!"

Perhaps one should not make too much of Errol's failure to pay debts. As we shall see, this young man was moving fast in a very fluid, almost frontier society. He undoubtedly was not the only individual who failed to tie up all the loose ends of his business affairs. Had he not become a screen idol known throughout the world his indebtedness (actual and imagined) would have been quickly forgotten. One suspects this link to a famous personality has given many residents of New Guinea, Papua, and Australia a ready (and much used) subject for beer conversation . . . although one of Errol's friends of those days claims he also spent freely when flush. She would maintain that, in the long run, his largess perhaps cancelled out any sums due those who yelled, "What about the money you owe me, Flynny?"

Actually, it is most unlikely that the "whole town" of Salamaua gathered to see local debtor make good. Regulations concerning native spectators at movies seem to have been capricious in the extreme. In 1927 the New Guinea administration issued an edict requiring a permit to show "cinematographic films". This permit might specifically forbid native attendance unless the films were educational, descriptive, travel, industrial, cartoons, of "general interest", or films in which all actors were natives. Five years later Sir Hubert Murray, whose bony, benevolent, blue-veined hands ruled Papua for several decades, told a newspaper reporter why no blacks were allowed in Port Moresby's lone cinema palace.

> These films often show white women in undignified roles and wearing little clothing. I regard these films as likely to bring white women into contempt.

Edmond Demaitre, who visited Rabaul on New Britain in the early 'thirties, found the New Guinea regulations of 1927 (which covered that region as well) still officially in force. He writes in *New Guinea Gold: Cannibals and Gold-Seekers in New Guinea* (London, 1936):

> Only certain selected films are shown, after strict censorship, to natives. The censors' task is not an easy one. They must suppress any reference to love-making, murder, robbery and crime in general, as well as war themes or the exploits of cowboys. The natives must not see a white woman being kissed, or a house being burgled, or how it is just as easy to kill a white man as a Kanaka. One can imagine how much of the film shown in Rabaul at half past six on Wednesday afternoons to a packed audience is left. There is a second show at nine in the evenings, but natives are not allowed to go to this performance which is given without cuts.

Yet, while chatting recently with a Sydney couple who lived in Lae in the 1930s, I asked if natives saw movies—wondering if indeed scores of black boys (and black girls, too!) who knew Errol Flynn ever saw him up there on the big screen. In unison he said "no" and she said "yes". It turned out that he meant they were barred and technically could not attend, More realistic, his wife conceded these truths but insisted blacks stood in the back and watched anyway. So much for government regulations concerning censorship of films . . . at least at Lae.

But, I get ahead of my story. The visit to New Guinea fired my interest in Errol Flynn, and upon my return to Sydney I began to dig deeper. I quickly learned he was born in Tasmania, had many associations with the Sydney area, and wrote three books. These are all clearly autobiographical and have a high fiction content even when classed as non-fiction. I say he *wrote* three books. He certainly was the author of the first two and dictated much of the third, although after his death it was prepared for publication by Earl Conrad, a well-known American writer who had been engaged for that specific purpose. Late in 1958 Conrad, now a San Francisco resident, spent some ten weeks working with Flynn at Port Antonio, Jamaica. All three books are invaluable guides to Errol's early years.

I would maintain that—wild and improbable as some of the tales in *Beam Ends, Showdown*, and *My Wicked, Wicked Ways* may at first appear—each episode contains at least a germ of truth. Nearly all of the events described were experienced to some degree by Flynn himself or by someone he knew well. And frequently one can pinpoint the true source without much difficulty.

A few hours with the *Sydney Morning Herald, Hobart Mercury, Rabaul Times*, and Port Moresby's *Papuan Courier* revealed one could indeed trace Errol's peregrinations in that corner of the world in the 1920s and early 1930s. Lists of ship passengers proved to be invaluable. Then came interviews and leads to more interviews, one tumbling fast upon another in quick succession.

Although it is impossible to thank everyone who has helped me piece this story together, I am especially grateful to Anthony Dell, Canberra (but of Tasmanian lineage); Mrs. Lillian Barclay Miller ("Tiger Lil"), Gold Coast; H. R. Niall, Lae; Lt. Col. J. Chapman, Hong Kong; Bill Penfold, Texas, Queensland; Eric F. Godward, Yackandandah, Victoria; John G. Gorton, Canberra; Merrick Long, Ashford, New South Wales; Francis N. Bell and Bob MacDonald, Brisbane; George Westacott and E. A. M. Palmer, Rockhampton; Miss Margaret Littlejohn, W. N. Oates, Mrs. Nancy Collis, J. K. Kerr, V. V. Hickman, and Mrs. C. G. Burton, all of Hobart; Mrs. Rosemary Flynn Warner, Washington, D.C.; Mr. and Mrs. Bert Weston, Stuart Inder (editor of the *Pacific Islands Monthly*), Neil E. Brook, Gavin Souter, Dr. Dexter Giblin, Dr. George Raudzens, Pat Eldershaw, Bjarne and Harold Halvorsen, John Warwick, Professor Ian Hogbin, Benedict Parer, Wallace Young, Mr. and Mrs. Allen Innes, Mrs. Charles

Chauvel, and Mr. and Mrs. Kenneth Hunter-Kerr, all of Sydney. Young and Hunter-Kerr provided numerous photos depicting Flynn's background and his life in the Sydney area.

While perhaps no consistent portrait of Errol Flynn emerges from discussion with those who knew him before he became famous—some individuals liked him and some didn't—there is universal agreement that he was a colorful, dynamic personality in his own right even before public relations boys and Hollywood sob sisters knew he existed. Many found his good looks and consummate arrogance offensive. Others were seduced by his natural charm and ready wit. Some were simply seduced.

Even if Errol Flynn had never reached Hollywood there are scores of people in Hobart, Sydney, Rockhampton, Port Moresby, Lae, Rabaul, and other communities where he spent the first half of his life who would still speak occasionally of that handsome, wayward rascal . . . "now what was his name?" But Errol *did* get to Hollywood, and therein lies the difference. His childhood pranks, teenage escapades, and adult adventures are well remembered, and so is his name.

I would like to thank these publishers for permission to quote from the following books and articles: Errol Flynn, *My Wicked, Wicked Ways* (New York: G. P. Putnam's Sons, 1959; London: William Heinemann Ltd., 1961); Tony Thomas, Rudy Behlmer, and Clifford McCarty, *The Films of Errol Flynn* (New York: Citadel Press, 1969); Elliott R. Thorpe, *East Wind, Rain* (Boston: Gambit, 1969); Edmond Demaitre, *New Guinea Gold: Cannibals and Gold-Seekers in New Guinea* (London: Geoffrey Bles, 1936); James Sinclair, *The Outside Man: Jack Hides of Papau* (Melbourne: Lansdowne Press, 1969); J. K. McCarthy, *Patrol Into Yesterday: My New Guinea Years* (Melbourne; Cheshire, 1963); Eric Feldt, "Errol Flynn at Salamaua", *Quadrant* (No. 20, Spring 1961); and seven letters which Flynn published in the Sydney *Bulletin* (1931-1932).

Several excerpts also are reproduced from Errol Flynn's *Beam Ends*, published by Cassell and Company of London in 1937; however, as the result of widespread destruction of business records during World War II, Cassell is unable to establish who holds copyright to this volume.

J.H.M.

\*

Chapter Eight, summarizing books published in recent decades describing the life of Errol Flynn, has been added to the original manuscript issued by Angus and Robertson in 1975.

# Chapter One

## An Education of Sorts—
## Formal, Informal, etc.

Errol Leslie Thomson Flynn was born on 20 June, 1909 at the Alexandra Private Hospital on Davey Street in Hobart, Tasmania. His parents, whose forbears had lived in New South Wales for several generations, moved to the picturesque capital of Australia's island state only a few weeks before his arrival. Errol's father, Theodore Thomson Flynn—tall, angular, rugged and scholarly—was born at Coraki in northern New South Wales on 11 October, 1883. He was educated at Sydney's famous Fort Street School, Sydney Teachers' Training College, and the University of Sydney. "Theo", as he was usually known, received his bachelor of science degree in 1906 along with the university medal in biology and the John Coutts Research Scholarship (£50). During the next two years he taught science, physics, and chemistry to high school students in the Newcastle-Maitland region a hundred or so miles north of Sydney.

In 1908 "Theo" married Lily Mary Young, a vivacious, beautiful young lady, one of six children, whom he perhaps met while a university student. Lily Mary, who later changed her name to Marelle (possibly to avoid confusion with Errol's first wife, Lili Damita . . . at least this is the theory of one relative) was the daughter of a diminutive fireball of a mother named Edith and a master mariner, George Young. One of Young's late eighteenth century relatives, a cousin or perhaps a great uncle, was Midshipman Edward Young who served aboard the *Bounty* and accompanied Fletcher Christian to Pitcairn Island. Lily Mary was born in North Sydney and grew up in and around that area. It is from the Youngs that Errol inherited much of his flair, good looks, and tempestuous ways. They were a roving lot, frequently earning their living at sea.

Leslie Young, the uncle who gave Errol one of his names, distinguished himself by winning a certificate and silver medal for saving two girls from drowning at National Park, N.S.W., in January of 1899. He was then only sixteen years old. Leslie, who later developed the Port Hacking Fisheries Hatchery, married Ethel Christian, a descendant of the *Bounty's* hero, and thus established a second link between the Youngs and that famous episode in naval annals. Errol writes that he and Uncle Les "hated each other's guts" and this was one reason he dropped the name; however, since Les died when Errol was a very small boy it seems unlikely that any true enmity ever existed.

Another of Lily Mary's brothers, Harry, was a distinguished marine engineer who served on numerous ships about the western Pacific. His son's home in the Drummoyne section of Sydney bears substantial evidence of those travels—intricate Chinese carvings, spears from the Solomon Islands, ship models, and other mementos of a life spent on the high seas. Prominent among these artifacts is a small wooden barrel about a foot long bound in heavy iron. This rum keg, which for many years graced the mantel at Grandma Young's home, once was used on the good ship *Bounty* to mete out grog rations. Pictures of Uncle Harry reveal an extremely handsome man, virtually the same profile which his nephew would someday project on movie screens throughout the world.

Less is known about Flynn's father's family, although it appears from his educational record that they must have moved from Coraki to Sydney sometime in the 1880s or '90s. When Errol was a youth his father's mother, a widow, lived at 28 Brighton Boulevard, Bondi—an eastern suburb famous for beach and surf.

In March of 1909, T. T. Flynn accepted a position lecturer in biology at the University of Tasmania. Thus Errol's debut in the shadows of Mount Wellington was not quite as haphazard as *My Wicked, Wicked Ways* might indicate. He has his parents steaming southward toward Antarctica on a scientific expedition; mother is found to be with Errol, and she is put ashore at Hobart while Theo continues on to unlock further mysteries of biological wonder. Not so. We will get to that expedition shortly: it occurred several years after Errol's birth. That Flynn was a bit confused about events during the first three or four years of his existence (and even prior to it) should surprise no one. All of us know that assorted facts and family lore often blend into a pleasant montage which becomes crystallized as fact alone. However, in Errol's case it is somewhat disturbing that this proclivity to weave a good tale began so very early and continued unabated for half a century!

There is little to indicate that Flynn's pre-school years were in any way out of the ordinary. He splashed or swam in the cool waters of Sandy Bay each summer, spent pleasant holidays with Sydney grandparents, and occasionally took a fleeting interest in his father's laboratory research. A sister, Rosemary, joined the family, and Theo's career prospered. In 1911 he was named Ralston Professor of Biology at the University of Tasmania, a post he held until 1931. In November of 1912 Professor Flynn joined Dr. Douglas Mawson in the *Aurora* for thirty-three days of oceanographic research in the waters off Macquarie Island 800 miles southeast of Tasmania. He was in charge of dredging and biological work. The Mawson Australasian Antarctic Expedition, an important scientific undertaking, lasted for three years (1911-14), and this excursion to Macquarie Island was only a small part of the total effort.

In 1915 Flynn became sole commissioner of fisheries for Tasmania and also began work on a higher degree at his alma mater, the University of Sydney. On 30 April, 1921, he received his doctorate in science, among the first awarded by that institution. His thesis, "The Foetal Membrane and Placentation of the Marsupialia", covers eighty-six pages and comes complete with an accompanying booklet of fifty-six photographs. For the unscientific, perhaps the most interesting aspect of this work is found in the introduction—a blunt outburst concerning the inability to consult vital biological literature in Hobart and "other disadvantages of isolation in Tasmania". This attitude, this revulsion toward an utterly beautiful but away-from-it-all island hidden under an almost equally isolated continent, was shared by Lily Mary as well. Accustomed to the pleasures and the excitement of metropolitan Sydney, she found Hobart provincial and boring.

It is difficult to conjecture as to what effect, if any, all this had upon Errol. He was young and Tasmania was his home, except for occasional visits to the mainland to see relatives. Yet, with his father busy in the laboratory and classroom and his mother far from happy with her geographical plight, a reaction of some sort may have been stirred within this youngster. He would have us believe that his rapport was always with his father and his constant antagonism with his mother. Perhaps. Anyone who has grown up in a home where dad was preoccupied with his job and the task of making a living while mother carried on the burden of family matters and meted out discipline will find this picture a familiar one. Nevertheless, we are dealing here with a very spirited little boy. He was highly intelligent, large for his age, handsome, and growing up in what, frankly, was not a co-ordinated, happy household.

Years later, a few weeks before Errol left New Guinea for Hong Kong and England, over many beers he told Benedict Parer of a childhood incident which, regardless of how much influence it may have had upon Errol, stunned his drinking companion. Parer, younger than Flynn and brought up in a large, devout Catholic family, found it impossible to accept Errol's apparent contempt for his mother and for women in general. Elements of this story are found in *My Wicked, Wicked Ways*.

At age seven or eight he got nabbed red-handed playing "you show me yours and I'll show you mine" with Nerida, a little girl who lived next door. (In 1971 I made inquiries in Hobart in a fruitless effort to locate Nerida.) Errol writes that this innocent introduction to sex, if we can call it that, was initiated by Nerida who was somewhat older than he was. Nerida's mother apprehended the pair with pants down and proceeded to let her little darling off with a mild reprimand. Lily Mary, on the other hand, lambasted the living hell out of her first born and later forced him to tell his father what he had done.

This confrontation became so heated that, as Errol tells us, he ran away from home for twenty-four hour to be greeted by wild maternal tears and unprecedented kisses when brought back. According to Parer, this story, as told to him at Mrs. Stewart's New Guinea pub, had a much more dramatic conclusion and more lasting impact. Errol, while saying nothing about his runaway adventure, told Parer that Lily Mary was so disgusted with his behavior that she referred to him as "pig . . . little pig" for nearly a year, refusing to call him by his Christian name. While perhaps an untrue tale, that Errol, age twenty-three, would tell it is in itself revealing.

During these years (1909-19) the Flynn's lived at several addresses in Hobart. The *Tasmanian Post Office Directory* reveals they were at 10 Darcy Street (1914-16), Holebrook Place (1917-18), and 60 Duke Street (1919). Errol began his formal education at the Franklin House School on Davey Street, but by 1918 was enrolled in the junior division of the Hutchins School, Hobart's most prestigious private, old-tie institution for miniature bluebloods. On the evening of 12 December, 1918, hair brushed and sitting straight, our little hero attended "Speech Night", the traditional closing exercises of the Hutchins school year held annually in the Hobart City

Hall. Headmaster C. C. Thorold, under the aristocratic gaze of Tasmania's royal governor, Sir Francis Newdegate, proclaimed that Hutchins had certainly done its part in the great war just ended. In firm tone he extolled the virtue and bravery of "old boys" who had answered the call of King and Country:

> Straight from leading football teams and captaining cricket elevens, straight from straining at an oar on behalf of their own much loved school, they went to play in a sterner way the same clean, true, earnest game, with all the pluck and indomitable determination which in the end—the long wished for glorious end—counted for victory. That Hutchins School played its part is proved by the fact that 247 old boys and three masters volunteered for active service. The toll, unfortunately, has been heavy, as 43 have made the supreme sacrifice. Their earthly warfare is closed, but their service and sacrifice will be commemorated as long as the school exists.

Thorold then disclosed plans for a memorial chapel, Newdegate presented prizes and awards (Errol was not a recipient), the school chorus sang a few numbers, and the evening closed with light refreshments.

A year later Errol sat through another "Speech Night", his last at Hutchins. The program was pretty much a re-run with Sir Francis praising scholarship, brave fighting men, the Empire, King George, and Tasmania . . . "a land of hope and glory—glory for its brilliant soldiers; hope from its great resources". Looking back over five decades it is difficult to know precisely what young Flynn, aged nine or ten, thought of these affairs; but if we conclude he was both bored and amused we would probably not be far off the mark. Considering the blunt analysis of Tasmania he heard around the dinner table at home he must have found this colonial, back-water nationalism pointless yet entertaining.

Errol lasted only one more term at Hutchins. (Australian schools traditionally operate on three terms of several months each from February to December.) In April of 1920 he entered Friends' School, a Quaker institution in North Hobart, and completed the year there. Several of his classmates remember him only as the large, precocious lad who taught them how to masturbate.

By 1921, as Errol was entering his twelfth year, basic elements of his personality were becoming discernible. He often appeared arrogant and self-assured, seemed capable of cruelty to animals, tended to be bored with classroom routine, and was contemptuous of authority in all forms. On the other hand, these unattractive qualities were more than balanced by considerable courtesy (when advantageous), wit, charm, and physical style. One Sydney relative, younger than Flynn, recalls he was "always a devil", a charge Errol himself would not deny since Part One of *My Wicked, Wicked Ways* bears the title of "The Tasmanian Devil, 1909-1927". According to this gentleman, the only way Lily Mary could discipline her wayward progeny was by pulling his hair. Spanking and more conventional methods had little effect.

From time to time Errol and other grandchildren gathered at Edith Young's place in Manly, a northern Sydney suburb. By this time Young himself had passed on and Grandma had married yet another huge man of the sea, Andrew Hammer. And it is Hammer, a cousin of the explorer Roald Amundsen, whom Flynn describes as his grandfather in his autobiography. Wallace Young, one of Edith's many grandchildren, remembers milk and bread breakfasts at "Grandma's" and several incidents which characterize his relationship with this Tasmanian cousin whom he thought virtually "uncontrollable". Theo maintained, by the way, that the milk and bread combination was "a very stable and ideal diet".

On one occasion the grandchildren, some of them very small, were on an outing in a rowboat belonging to Charlie Sly, a neighbor. Errol, a teenage show-off, attempted to upset the craft and was ordered out of the boat by the owner. That night Errol cut some reeds, sharpened the ends, and ran them through Sly's fishing catch which was crated and ready for the Sydney market, thus destroying several days work. Another time, when Hammer's five-masted schooner, the *H. K. Hall*, was in port, excited youngsters swarmed over the vessel. In short order the boy who would become Captain Blood a decade later was swinging in the rigging with loud shouts and much bravado. Summoned back to the deck, he sulked for a few moments; then, when no one was looking, he threw all the buckets used by the crew over the side.

Young also recalls the first of numerous flimflam deals which his cousin would pull so frequently on credulous associates. A Manly storekeeper who lived near Grandmother Young's home paid a small sum for each soft drink bottle returned to him. These were then stacked in a back yard which was enclosed by a secure fence. However, our cunning little lad pried a board loose, picked up armfuls of bottles, and carried them around to the store. He made a juvenile killing . . . that is, until apprehended.

About 1920 the Hammers moved to 54 Carabella Street, Kirribilli, a North Sydney suburb much closer to the heart of the metropolitan area. It is this address which Errol remembers as his grandmother's home in his autobiography. In the mid-twenties the Hammers were living at 279 Avoca Street, Randwick, an eastern suburb, where Andrew—in his last years and retired from the sea—busied himself with dreams of a fortune made from his franchise of the Burpee Self-Canner, a Yankee innovation.

Sometime in the early 1920s Errol and his father sailed for England. They probably departed from Melbourne during the last half of 1921, stopped briefly in South Africa, and then continued on to London. The precise date of this trip is not known. Records at the University of Tasmania indicate Professor Flynn spent much time in Sydney doing research. In April of 1921, the month he received his doctorate, he wrote to University officials from that city, and the following month informed them he would like to spend the period from September 1922 to March 1923 in either Melbourne or Sydney. In August of 1923 he represented Tasmania at the Pan-Pacific Conference held in Sydney and a month later sailed for London, arriving there late in October.

Just where young Errol was during these years is something of a mystery. He obviously was not attending school in Hobart, although it is apparent he returned form England with his father in June 1924. In *My Wicked, Wicked Ways* he says he spent "two of the most dismal years of my life" at South-West London College, a primary school between Putney and Hammersmith. Flynn then spins on for several pages describing an existence which even Oliver Twist would not envy—homosexual masters, lousy food, neglected and forgotten by his parents. He tells us his father was busy researching and making new scientific discoveries at the University of London or doing much the same thing back in Australia. Meanwhile, his mother and her sister Betty, who had followed Flynn and his father to England, were having a high old time in Paris . . . and Theo was not doing too badly either.

While his family was abroad Professor Flynn's professional and social careers prospered. He continued publication of a series of scholarly biological reports which brought him considerable repute. In all, he produced twenty-eight papers between 1909 and 1931, most of them printed in Tasmania. "Prof." Flynn, as he was called by students, also gave fencing and Morris (Welsh) dancing lessons to elite young ladies of Hobart during the early 1920s and was, according to one former student, "a proper gentleman at all times, a very proper gentleman indeed! Yet rumor indicates that T. T. was beginning to demonstrate some of the romantic proclivities which his son would soon develop into a fine art. One Sydney woman even got a divorce expecting the professor to do likewise. However, this is hardly surprising considering he was a large healthy specimen of manhood aged about forty with a wife away in Europe for months, perhaps years at a time.

Back in jolly old England Errol was, as usual, in trouble. He writes in his autobiography that in his fifteenth year he was expelled from South-West London College; but, because he was Professor Flynn's son, he gained immediate admission to nearby Colet Court, a preparatory school for St. Paul's (founded 1509). He tells us he did not remain at Colet Court long; however, these experiences later become part of *Showdown*. Young Shamus O'Thames, the hero, spends "two desperately lonely years" with a private tutor in Devon named Burbidge . . . almost the same name, according to Flynn, as that of the headmaster (Burbridge) at cheerless South-West London College.

Flynn's autobiographical entry in *Who's Who in Australia* (1959) lists St. Paul's and South-West London College, but fails to mention any of the Tasmanian schools he attended (there is one more to come and another in Australia as well). His entry in *Who's Who in America* (1952-3) cites the two British preparatory schools and throws in "King's School (Ireland)" for good measure. Of course, this may be merely a public relations gambit to exploit the fake Irish background so dear to the hearts of Warner Brothers. To add to this confusion, there is no South-West London College listed in the *London Post Office Directory* (1923) or in any guides to British preparatory schools published during those years. As for St. Paul's, letters of inquiry sent to that august institution have gone unanswered.

On 14 July, 1924, Errol enrolled in Hobart High School's second year class. He gave his address as Pressland House and cited "South-West College, London as the last school attended, having left that institution in April 1924. Pressland House at 33 Melville Street, Hobart, began life as a private school in the 1840s, but was now a well-known boarding house. It still exists (1971) in a run-down condition. A letter of Errol's reproduced in *My Wicked, Wicked Ways* indicates his father was living there in 1930. So, one can assume this was "home for both Errol and the professor as long as they continued to have anything to do with Hobart and Tasmania. Once his mother saw Europe it appears that she was most reluctant to return Down Under and only made spasmodic visits to Sydney.

If Errol's meanderings are confusing, so are those of his mother and sister Rosemary, born in 1920. For several years during that decade, apparently accompanied by her infant daughter, Mrs. Flynn was part of the Aga Khan's famed entourage. When asked in the 1970s how and why her parents were re-united, Rosemary (who knew little about her brother's pre-film career) replied, "It's all quite simple. Mummy just ran out of money."

Arrival at Hobart High, a state school lacking the polish of Hutchins and Friends, hardly went unnoticed nor was it Errol's intention that it should. This is how one student (female) remembers that dramatic moment:

> He arrived one morning while the boys in the class were at physics & as prefect in D class (2nd year) I was instructed by the then headmaster, Mr. P. H. Mitchell, to introduce him to class and teacher & attend to any necessary formalities. He was then 15 years old; just over six feet and incredibly good-looking, dressed in Eton-type clothes—striped morning trousers, short black coat, white shirt, and bow tie. He was also incredibly smug and contemptuous of the rather hardworking, ambitious class in which he was placed.

It doesn't take much imagination to realize what Hobart High boys thought of this strange apparition. (Errol sometimes spread the tale that he actually attended Eton while living in England.) Nor does one have to ponder long the effect of this "incredibly good-looking six-footer upon Hobart High girls. According to the lady who recalls this theatrical entrance, "He quickly formed a romantic attachment for a pretty blonde girl in the A class!" Nearly half a century later she remains somewhat shocked that a fifteen-year-old boy would dare to date an older woman; but, at least until he got into his thirties, Errol always demonstrated a marked preference for mature, experienced females. Then, as we all know, having gained experience himself, he decided to become teacher.

To promote this high school romance Errol asked the D class prefect who had introduced him about Hobart High to deliver notes to the pretty blonde. As a result he was soon escorting the object of his current desires to "the pictures" at the Strand Theatre. And the prefect-cum-courier recalls:

> Quite a party of the girls in our class delighted to sit en bloc in the seats behind them, to his consequent rage. In those distant days attendance at this theatre on Saturday afternoons was the 'in' thing. It cost us 6½d., but Errol sat in the Lounge (1/1).

During these weekend outings Errol, his blonde, and their noisy pack of entranced on-lookers saw such wonders as Milton Sills and Anna Q. Nilsson in *The Spoilers*, Jackie Coogan in *Little Robinson Crusoe*, and Tom Mix in *Dick Turpin*. They also watched the smooth operations of Ramon Navarro (*The Arab* and *What I Want I Take!*), Adolph Menjou (*A Kiss in the Dark*), Rudolph Valentino (*The Sainted Devil*), and Ronald Colman (*His Supreme Moment*). A decade or so later Flynn would be associating with some of these Hollywood personalities (if they survived the advent of sound), and Hobart youngsters—snuggling in the same seats at the Strand—could watch as a hometown boy became Captain Peter Blood, Robin Hood, and the Earl of Essex.

Errol completed the school year of 1924 at Hobart High and was enrolled there during 1925 as well. Until late in the second year nothing out of the ordinary seems to have occurred. He went about his lessons in a haphazard manner and continued that "picture show romance". On one occasion, when informed that the young female prefect who carried his love letter had said he was "a perfect example for an advertisement for soap", she herself received a Flynn note: "If your mother had used more soap on you, your hair might not be so red and your tongue so tart!"

Then Errol suddenly wound up his Tasmanian career with a remarkable flourish—an athletic triumph of substantial import cheek to jowl with a bit of silly horseplay which appears quite juvenile for a strapping, six-foot sixteen-year-old. Yet anyone who thinks back to his own high school days can remember the fierce internal battle that raged between proper and improper conduct, between adult and childish ways.

In October, as a member of Hobart's "northern" tennis team, Errol fought his way to the finals of intra-city club play. On 2 November he was the only " northerner" to win against "southern" competition. He beat a player named Fysh 5-6 [*sic*], 6-3, 6-3 in what the *Hobart Mercury* said was "the best tennis of the day" at the New Town courts.

In the city class B semi-finals on 25 November Errol, representing his Fernside Club, was extremely impressive against C. O. Turner—5-6, 6-4, 6-3:

> The match between Flynn, the Fernside junior, and Turner, of Buckingham, was a fine contest, E. T. Flynn eventually winning in the third set. The tennis throughout was the best witnessed to date. Turner started off with drives of good length, followed by splendid drop-volleys at net. This at first baffled Flynn, who was having his best drives dropped over the net for winners, but by altering his game altogether and cutting crisply to each side-line, Flynn eventually forced Turner to the

baseline, where he had little difficulty in out-driving the last named.

Five days later Errol beat a player named Morey (6-3, 6-4) to clinch a finals berth; and, on Saturday, 5 December, he met B. Scoles at New Town. It was very warm, "excessively so", but a large crowd of tennis enthusiasts turned out and they were well rewarded.

Flynn commenced strongly, and by clean and forceful good length driving kept his opponent in the back court, quickly running to a lead of 4-1. Though Scoles had some good recoveries he was unable to deal with the pace of Flynn's shots, and the Fernsider took the set in two games. Scoles took the offensive at the commencement of the second set, and, coming to the net frequently, made many winning volleys, his driving, too, being much steadier than formerly. Flynn, on the other hand, lost a bit of his accuracy during this set, and the Buckingham representative evened the score. Both players were by this time glad to take advantage of the usual respite, and on resumption a neck-and-neck struggle ensued until the score was four all. At that stage Flynn, by superior play, took the next two games, thereby gaining the rubber, and with it the title of B grade champion for the year.

A few days later Hobart's junior tennis king decided to put some sparkle into the first and only school fair ever held at Hobart High. Errol and the head prefect, "a hitherto earnest, dependable type", bought ice creams which they took into a gallery and dropped onto the heads of people on the main floor beneath them. Banished from the fete by Headmaster Mitchell, a somewhat fussy man in the opinion of one of Flynn's classmates, Errol compounded his evening of infamy by spreading treacle (molasses) around the steering wheel of Mitchell's car. An hour or so later the headmaster emerged from the fair and climbed into his vehicle. If splattering ice cream had not been sufficient cause, the sticky mess he found definitely delivered the coup de grâce.

Concerning Flynn's demise the little red-headed prefect has this to say:

> He left the school in December suddenly and unexpectedly. In those reticent days misdeeds and indiscretions were never made public, but we all knew he had been 'asked to leave' as the result of a contretemps on the evening of the only fair H. H. S. ever experienced.

Official school records reveal that E. T. Flynn and Hobart High severed relations on 16 December, 1925. Errol had completed C class or his third year of high school education.

Summing up her memories of the future screen idol, the prefect concludes,

> Naturally we, his class, followed his future career with great interest. His character was dominated by a contempt for convention and a desire to shock. He was the complete egotist. His extreme good looks were spoilt by an incredibly smug expression, plainly seen in his pictures.

On 23 January, 1926, Professor Flynn left Hobart on the *Riverina* bound for Sydney. Early in March Errol made the same trip to begin his classes at a famous Australian school. It proved yet another unsuccessful assault upon the proud tower of learning. Somehow T. T. had convinced L. C. Robson, the austere headmaster of Sydney Church of England Grammar School (SCEGS), that his son deserved one more chance.

Robson—B. Sc. (Sydney), M.A. (Oxon.), Rhodes Scholar from New South Wales (1916), Lieutenant, 18th Battalion A.I.F. (1915-19), first class final honors at Oxford (1920)—directed the fortunes of SCEGS, usually called simply "Shore", from 1923 to 1958. He was always, and perhaps with good reason, somewhat more interested in turning out gentlemen first and scholars second. Viewed in this light Errol's academic record was not so frightening. He actually had progressed well enough despite years in England and a disclination to study. And he most certainly *looked* like a gentleman, even if clearly not a scholar. To Robson's horror he would soon discover the "Tasmanian Devil" was neither.

Pat Eldershaw, a young English master who had joined the Shore staff two years earlier, recalls Errol's arrival at the North Sydney School. Eldershaw was in charge of School House, the residence hall to which Flynn was first assigned; however, a few hours later he was moved to Robson House. Someone had made an error, much to the dismay of the matron of School House: "Imagine it! They've taken that good-looking Tasmanian boy away from us!" Like Robson, within a few weeks she too learned that Flynn's appearance was most deceptive.

Years later when Shore was organizing a drive for funds the staff met to consider likely donors. Eldershaw said he thought he knew an old boy who might help out *if* they could get him interested. Robson at once asked who that might be. The name of Errol Flynn was greeted with a frozen stare from the headmaster. No more was heard of that suggestion. Eldershaw, a jovial man with a delightfully puckish sense of humor, says whenever the Shore boys get a bit too full of themselves at reunion gatherings he reminds them that in his career at SCEGS he had the pleasure of teaching "two murderers and Errol Flynn".

Like other boys in his form Errol took English, French, math, history, chemistry, and physics. Whether one can call this a "course of study" is questionable; although Flynn certainly learned more while doing his English composition exercises than he might admit. His writing of later years proves this to be true. However, this restless student seems to have spent an inordinate amount of his time at compulsory drill, detention, and athletics. This is how Bill Penfold, a Queensland grazier, remembers his former classmate.

Errol was a beautifully built & proportioned boy, a mature 16 or 17 at school, to me and I would say to the other boys a thoroughly likeable chap. There was no particular vice in him, in fact I would say contra, if a small bud was being bullied it would be Errol that would kick the bigger bud's pants. His acting & appearance (of a later date) would be perfectly natural, his looks & bearing were the same at school as later pictures showed. He was in the school's first term teams & I think won the light heavyweight class at boxing, his football to us was a bit spectacular, not being used to Australian Rules, but his marking & drop kicking were beautiful to watch. I don't know what grade of football he made. Again, as a cricketer, I don't remember beyond the fact that he was always on for a game of French cricket during the play period. I can also remember he copped his fair share of Friday afternoon drills & Saturday morning detentions, mainly caused by his somewhat supercilious attitude with the masters. I liked him very much, as did most buds of those days.

Francis N. Bell, then senior boy at Robson House, recalls how the headmaster asked him to look after the new boarder.

I arranged for Errol to sit near me at my table at meals and I found out very soon from him that he had apparently rowed quite a lot. I asked him to come down to the boat sheds as we were always on the lookout for any likely looking rowers. When he was asked to go out in a tub pair at the shed, it was clearly apparent that he had never been in a rowing boat in his life! This was the first of many more blatant lies told by Errol.

Other old boys paint a somewhat different picture. When contacted several were not even aware that they were at Shore with Errol Flynn. One who remembered him and specifically asked to remain anonymous, said he was big for his age, "close to six feet, broad shoulders, a little bit flabby and certainly not in football condition". Several factors may help to explain such comments There were nearly 500 students at the school in 1926. Flynn arrived "new" after friendships of long standing had been forged; and, since activities centered about each residence house, it is not unusual that many students rarely knew boys outside of their own established circle. According to Eldershaw, Flynn dressed very well but always seemed to lack spending money. It was, he notes, as if his parents outfitted him, put him in school, and then forgot about him.

The *Torch-Bearer*, a small magazine published each term by SCEGS, reports "Flynn, E. L. T." entered the school in March of 1926. His entrance number was 3955. He played successful tennis, making the first team and winning "third award", and participated in house cricket. And, as Penfold and Eldershaw observed, Flynn also played football (having grown up with the Australian Rules version favored in Tasmania and Victoria as opposed to Rugby Union played in New South Wales private schools); and, according to some individuals, he boxed superbly.

Eldershaw says Flynn once saw one of the schools leading boxers heading toward the gymnasium with several pairs of gloves in hand. They got to chatting. Errol tagged along, put on the mitts just for the fun of it, and promptly belted his opponent so hard that workmen had to repair the wall where he landed. John G. Gorton, former Prime Minister of Australia, was also at Robson House in 1926. Gorton, somewhat younger than the big Tasmanian, says he did not have "any close contact" with Flynn, adding, "I do remember him as a first class boxer." However, Francis Bell, a seasoned campaigner himself, thought Error only "fair" in the ring. A decade later, to promote *The Perfect Specimen*, a movie made with Joan Blondell, Hugh Herbert, Edward Everett Horton, and May Robson, Warner Brothers spread the hoax that Flynn boxed in the 1928 Olympics held at Amsterdam.

Yet, despite athletic success, the friendship and admiration of numerous classmates, and a mediocre-to-lousy classroom performance, Errol was booted out of Shore late in the second term, probably in August of 1926. The root of the trouble was a sexual itch which, during the next thirty years, would cause Flynn considerable pleasure and pain and bring him fame, fortune, headlines, and grief. In *My Wicked, Wicked Ways* he describes a knockdown brawl with the school bully (a youth named "Lindsay", although no such surname appears in the SCEGS records of those years) and their jealous competition for the favors of a maid named Elsie. He says his relationship with Elsie was non-sexual. Shortly after the fight Robson summoned Flynn to his office and expelled him for being "a disturbing influence on the rest of the scholars". While the headmaster may have used those words both of them knew Flynn was being asked to leave because he was a disturbing influence upon Elsie, not on his fellow scholars. To them he was, in fact, an inspiration . . . a man among boys.

According to several associates "Flynn, E. L. T." was apprehended on the school's coal pile with the daughter of the laundress. Whether her name was Elsie is anyone's guess. As one classmate put it,

> His dismissal from school was not for bad influence on the boys, but for rooting one of the maids. I can still visualize her—a strong, thick-set girl about 19 years old with brushed back hair & quite plain.

Another version of Errol's expulsion from Shore also exists, although—as is so often the case with this young man's career—the details do not differ greatly and the outcome is the same. One senior boy, conceding Flynn was "really a charming chap to meet with a wonderful smile and great personality", remembers l'affaire coal pile but says another incident led directly to his departure. Commenting on the future star's athletic prowess he notes:

As far as tennis was concerned he showed good ability but unfortunately it was his undoing as he was caught stealing money from one of the guests at a party given by a member of the school tennis team and expelled from the school.

It is impossible to say what would have shocked Headmaster Robson more—stealing or screwing. Perhaps it was simply a matter of one misdeed falling hot on the heels of another and complicated by a lackluster academic record. Whatever the sequence of events, these episodes seem quite in character. Errol always was out for a fast buck (Eldershaw said he had no spending money); and, as all the world knows, he *was* a fast buck as well!

One friend says Robson was so distressed by whatever Flynn did that he demanded he pack and be gone. Errol was not even permitted to stay for lunch following the morning confrontation. And dismissal was thoroughly complete. Although school records extend back to the first student, the present registrar has no file on Flynn, and his name is missing from a meticulously constructed list of old boys published in the late 1920s. *The Register of the Sydney Church of England Grammar School—July, 1889, to December, 1926* simply ignores the existence of the young man who would become that institution's most famous alumnus. This summary compiled by the chaplain of that era skips from Flecknoe (3954) to Ford (3956)—Flynn and his number 3955 do not appear on page 311. He thus joins a very select group. Only five other numbers are missing from this compendium.

So eight or ten weeks after his seventeenth birthday Errol's troubled school career came to an end. He tells us in *My Wicked, Wicked Ways* that he was a mere waif all alone in Australia—father in England, mother in France. Things actually were not that bleak. He had two grandmothers who worshipped him, aunts and uncles, numerous cousins, and several influential acquaintances, all living in the Sydney area.

Errol first went to his grandmother Flynn's place at Bondi where he would live from time to time during the next few years. He then sought out a handsome young businessman by the name of Kenneth Hunter-Kerr who would have substantial influence upon his life from 1926 to 1933. Hunter-Kerr, now semi-retired but busily engaged as a model, was somewhat older than Errol. He doesn't remember precisely how or when they met . . . "probably on the beach through mutual friends, I guess". For reasons best known to Flynn this engaging benefactor is not mentioned in his autobiography.

The first task was to find Errol a job. Hunter-Kerr and his father put their heads together and decided to contact Sir Henry Braddon who managed Dalgety and Company Limited, a huge shipping and merchandise concern which specialized in export of agricultural produce (especially wool) and import of a multitude of goods—automobiles, sheep dip, cigars, wines, and spirits. Braddon, Australia's first commercial commissioner in America (1918-19), or some member of his staff put Errol to work in the general mail section in September 1926. He said he was eighteen (a year older than he actually was) and gave his address as 28 Brighton Boulevard, Bondi—grandma Flynn's home.

Among his co-workers was Neil E. Brook, a year or so younger, who obviosuly idolized the handsome Tasmanian youth. Brook found him enterprising, alert, athletic. Once a "grade A" table tennis player himself, he says Flynn usually beat him at that sport all too easily. They became especially good friends when they worked side by side in Dalgety's Wharf and Stevedoring Department at Miller's Point, Flynn having been transferred there on 26 June, 1927, a few days after his eighteenth birthday.

During these months Errol's social life also prospered, thanks to Ken Hunter-Kerr with whom he lived during occasional spats with grandma. Ken, a dashing young socialite, had a small cottage in King's Cross where a large motel now stands. "The Cross" of the 1970s is sort of a mini Greenwich Village-Times Square, a honky-tonk Down Under known to thousands of American R and R men who visited Australia from Vietnam, but in the late 1920s it was still largely residential. At Hunter-Kerr's home Flynn met a collection of wealthy young belles, nearly all of them slightly older than he was since they were actually Ken's circle of friends.

Of prime importance in this group were the Dibbs girls—Miriam, Naomi, and Cecile, the daughters of Mr. and Mrs. R. Campbell Dibbs of Bowral and Temora. Their grandfather, Sir Thomas Allwright Dibbs, was general manager of Sydney's Commercial Banking Company from 1867 to 1915. His brother, Sir George R. Dibbs, was a political power in New South Wales in the 1880s and 1890s, serving two terms as premier and holding other important government positions. Several years later Errol became engaged to Naomi for a time, and in January of 1932 Ken Hunter-Kerr married Miriam. Other members of this smart little set included Phyl McLauchlan (Lady Collins, wife of Vice-Admiral Sir John Augustine Collins), Edward Ashley Cooper, his sister Enid, and Bradley Ryrie, son of Major General Sir Granville de Laune Ryrie. Cooper subsequently gained prominence under the abbreviated stage name of Ashley Cooper.

With this group Errol danced, drank, swam, played tennis and occasionally drove at breakneck speeds between parties in Sydney and Bowral, some eighty miles southwest of the metropolitan area. Debonair, handsome, witty, superb on the tennis court, he was a natural recruit to their ranks. Yet, to some degree, Flynn was in over his depth. He was a lad of seventeen or eighteen traveling with a very well-to-do crowd on a clerk's salary; and, while his disdain for social convention might at first be thought amusing, the establishment's offspring can tire quickly of such outbursts . . . and their parents *very* quickly indeed!

On Thursday evening, 25 August, 1927, Errol Flynn entered the ring at Sydney Stadium as a contender in the New South Wales state amateur boxing competition. He was eliminated by a heavier opponent, but apparently performed in an impressive fashion. "Solar Plexus" wrote in the *Referee* (31 August):

> In the heavyweight division, E. Flynn (11.10) beat F. Scarf (12.10) by a margin as wide as the Sydney Heads. But both judges agreed for Scarf who did not land a decent blow owing to the other fellow's elusiveness, or straight left worked overtime, if lightly. In the last round, the only hard blow by Flynn, a right swing, momentarily dazed his bigger and stronger, but infinitely less scientific opponent.

A few days later "Solar Plexus" reported that Scarf was also eliminated, and he added with delight, "The loser will be well advised to stick to the grappling game". It might be worth noting that old Shore boys who faced Errol in the ring remember he had one bit of deadly deception. As he danced about in front of you smiling contemptuously he occasionally glanced down at his feet. In time, almost a reflex action, you would do the same—and that was when the blow fell.

However, on the day that the *Referee* praised Errol's ring style the "blow" fell on him. He was summarily dismissed from Dalgety's. Brook says Flynn just disappeared and fellow workers were told he would not be back. It seems Errol's department was deeply involved in the shipment of goods to Fiji, Dalgety's being purchasing agent for that colony in Sydney. Our lad apparently played loose with a substantial sum from the stamp account in order to buy a bicycle . . . and got caught. As a current Dalgety executive commented while discussing this episode, "Many an office boy has come to grief over petty (and not so petty) cash accounts." *My Wicked, Wicked Ways* tells a somewhat different tale, but theft is admitted and the result is the same—fired. Ken Hunter-Kerr stoutly maintains that this is one escapade which was settled in full. The bicycle was returned to the shop where Errol bought it, and the money due Dalgety's was paid to them. In his autobiography Flynn next regales us with stories of nights spent on park benches and life with bums during September of 1927. Considering the hospitality of Hunter-Kerr and the devotion of two grandmothers who adored him, this sounds far fetched.

But once more, almost a year to the day since being expelled from Shore, Errol was out in the cold. What to do? He spent about three weeks in and around Sydney, perhaps learning that without references from his previous employer white collar jobs were hard to find. Then, not surprisingly, his eyes turned northward toward New Guinea. Fortunes were being scooped out of the black earth up there. Newspapers overflowed with stories of sudden wealth. A Rabaul accountant visiting Adelaide declared the surface had only been "scratched". It was possible the gold fields in the mountains in back of Salamaua on New Guinea's northern coast would prove to be "the greatest alluvial discovery of modern times". In March of 1927 the *Melusia* arrived in Sydney with 14,000 ounces of yellow metal, the largest shipment yet.

Late in September, with visions of sudden riches dancing in his head, Errol Flynn boarded the *Montoro* bound for Rabaul, the gateway to New Guinea. Where his passage money came from is something of a mystery. He says Naomi hurled her engagement ring at him during a quarrel (they were not engaged until January of 1931), it rolled under a piano, and he squirmed after it. Sale of this jewelry plus a loan from "Uncle Oscar" (whoever he was) gave him the £18 needed for a ticket. He tells us in *My Wicked, Wicked Ways* that all of this occurred "early in 1926" when he was "only seventeen". Well, Errol has the fare right even if attendant details are somewhat muddled and confused.

# Chapter Two

## Drifter in Paradise, 1927-1929

The island world which welcomed young Errol Flynn is fully as exotic as those who have never seen it believe it to be. It was a land of tremendous contrast and captivating beauty in the 1920s and, despite war, progress (?), and change, remains so half a century later. As nearly as anyone can tell, the handsome youngster who arrived in Rabaul on 1 October, 1927, spent the following twenty-five months in a number of jobs, frequently getting the boot or suddenly quitting after only a few weeks. Part of his problem was undoubtedly endemic teenage restlessness, but this urge was complicated by well-developed laziness, contempt for authority, and—very frankly—failure to get enough sleep each night. Involved with cards, drink, or perhaps some romantic exploit if the opportunity presented herself, Errol's employers got short shrift indeed.

The locale of these adventures, if one can so term them, was the islands of New Britain, New Ireland, and New Guinea. And our hero appears to have tarried from time to time on some of the lesser outlying islands as well . . . Umboi, New Hanover, and Lemus, for example. In the 1920s the three major land masses differed greatly. New Ireland, stretching some 220 long, narrow miles, had been almost completely subdued by Teutonic efficiency prior to 1914. Well-tended plantations, fine highways, and smiling natives were the earmark of that region. Lying to the south was New Britain, a land of volcanoes and rugged terrain contaminated by mere enclaves of European civilization. Steaming Rabaul, capital of the Australian League of Nations mandate which encompassed all three islands, gave New Britain a transitory importance. It was the transport-mercantile hub of the area and, until nearby mountains blew their tops in 1937 and the ravages of Japanese occupation and war added to the devastation, a centre of considerable activity.

Mandated New Guinea, actually only the northeastern quarter of the huge island sprawling southwest of New Britain and hovering over the Australian continent like a giant bird, rounds out the arc of colonies once ruled by Kaiser Wilhelm II. However, the New Guinea which would occasionally get glimpses of young Flynn (and vice versa) differed greatly from the neighboring islands. It was more rugged, almost entirely jungle or high plateaus and towering mountains. There were no highways and few white settlers. Conveniences common to New Ireland and sometimes found in parts of New Britain were unknown.

Yet the forbidding mass of New Guinea, shared with the Dutch to the west and the Australian colony of Papua to the south, had something the other islands lacked—*gold*, and within a few years that yellow metal would create a unique frontier which hurdled from cannibalism to air travel in a single bound. Roads, cities, trams, railways, all of those adornments which decorate the orderly progress of white man's cultural-material growth were lacking. In fact, in 1927, the year that Errol stepped off onto a Rabaul wharf, regular air service was inaugurated between the Lae-Salamaua area on New Guinea's north coast and the rich Wau-Bulolo gold fields some fifty miles inland. Within five years the Lae airport would become one of the busiest in the world. In time, as Flynn spun his way through a swift kaleidoscope of occupations, he even became an employee of one of these pioneer transport companies. But, first to Rabaul, the port where he began his island career.

Edmond Demaitre, a gifted French writer who visited New Britain in the early 1930s, has left us a clear (if cynical) portrait of life there. His delightful *New Guinea Gold: Cannibals and Gold-Seekers in New Guinea* (London, 1936) describes the society in which Errol moved for a time. There were, Demaitre notes, less than 4,000 non-blacks in the entire mandate in 1929. This total includes 1,808 British citizens, 1,253 Chinese, 328 Germans, 213 Dutch, and 41 French.

In Rabaul itself he found a culture based upon three sturdy foundations dear to the hearts of Englishmen everywhere: the Empire, the Bible, and Tea. There was the traditional Anglican church and the traditional dull club; and, despite oppressive heat, Demaitre concluded Rabaul was a bit like any provincial town be it in Australia, Canada, Sussex, or Hampshire.

There is a tennis-court, a golf course, shady avenues, where one rides on Sundays, a chemist's shop, a hospital, a law court, a tea-shop, two hotels, three restaurants, two clubs, churches, cemeteries, a library, lawyers, doctors, odd-looking officials, old women who know all about everything, schoolmasters, a journalist, women who are misunderstood, men who are bored, family gatherings, marriages arranged, dinners, and evening parties, at which girls write down the names of their partners on a program with an illuminated heading of mauve turtle doves. The men keep a top hat and moth-eaten frock coat in tin lined wardrobes, the women think and talk of the marvelous time they had in Sydney and Melbourne, the girls flirt with their fathers' secretaries and assistants, in expectation of the time when the young man may get promoted and an increase in pay which will enable him to marry. At the little music hall the usual frequenters are there in force: the people one does not call on, the well-informed person, the incorrigible Don Juan, the woman who deceives her husband, and the man who drinks because he is unhappy.

The town is picturesque. It is tucked away in a little valley opening on to the sea between green hills. With its white bungalows half hidden behind the thick foliage of poplars, coconut palms and strange trees resembling the cassowary, with its broad avenues bordered by beds of exotically-scented flowers, with its extinct volcano at the back, looking like a cross old hunchback, with its rock-strewn beach, where the emerald waters of the Pacific come to rest, Rabaul gives the impression of being an earthly Paradise. At night a fresh breeze caresses the tall trunks of the palm trees, roosting birds rustle in the leaves, and giant turtles emerge from the sea and crawl slowly over the sand which glistens in the moonlight.

While the town seemed picturesque and ostensibly carefree, Demaitre concedes it was plagued by two problems, twin clouds which hung over the region like a dark pall: malaria and a craving for the gold of the New Guinea highlands. Errol Flynn would soon be infected by both. And there was yet another problem which Demaitre failed to appreciate. That cross old hunchback of a volcano still had a lot of zip left in him!

Issues of the *Rabaul Times* for 1927 indicate that this picture of the island community was essentially true. In September of that year the twelve-page weekly boasted that both Burns Philp and W. R. Carpenter (leading shipping concerns maintaining contact with Australia and the outside world) could supply Buick, Ford, and Chevrolet cars, trucks of various makes, Heidsieck champagne, Gilbey's gin, a variety of tinned meats, beer, lager, engines, oil, petrol, etc. If of proper social class one could play cricket and tennis or swim at the local club. Christmas season promised race meets, and Kwong Foo Lung's store advertised the Dulcitone piano, only sixty pounds of highly polished, imitation oak or mahogany that "never needs tuning".

There was a resident dentist, literary and debating societies met monthly, and one could dance each Saturday evening to the strains of the Tropical Troubadours at the Kokopo Hotel a dozen miles across Blanche Bay from Rabaul. Mrs. Winter's

Theatre Cafe offered breakfast 7-9, lunch 12-1:30, dinner, 6-7:30, "the best food in the territory at the usual price". Large display ads hailed "Standard" boots as best for the gold fields, and native misdemeanors were listed, euphemistically, under the weekly heading inspired by Rudyard Ripling and others: "White Man's Burden".

These gleanings from the local newspaper, the only one published in the mandate, and random observations by Edmond Demaitre give some insight into the kind of community Errol Flynn found in New Britain's largest port late in 1927. Despite the French writer's emphasis upon propriety, it was actually a raucous, swinging South Sea whore of a town, but certainly not primitive, head-hunting jungle. Natives had been subdued or pushed into the background, their nocturnal movements circumscribed by a rigid pass system; and a weak veneer of British-Australian culture, a semblance of what had been left behind, strove valiantly to create a miniature Sydney or Brisbane.

The thin white line, in this instance bolstered by scores of diligent yellow merchants, did what it could to uphold God, good King George, cold Queen Mary, and the Anglo-Saxon heritage. For a brief time those manning the ramparts of righteousness saw young E. L. T. Flynn as a likely recruit to their ranks; but, within weeks, some had doubts about the basic stability of this dashing Tasmanian youth of good family.

Errol arrived in Rabaul aboard the *Montoro*, a Burns Philp steamer. Fellow passengers included a public servant named Johnson who, as Flynn tells us in *My Wicked, Wicked Ways*, may have helped him become a cadet patrol officer. It is also possible that E. W. P. Chinnery—government anthropologist, a friend of his father, and whose name Flynn butchers as "Chimery" and "Channery"—was instrumental in getting him into a neat, white uniform. However, he was soon out of it.

In 1925 the Australian government inaugurated a cadet program to train young men as patrol officers, those hardy souls who represent central authority among Papua-New Guinea tribes to the present day. Each youth was to undergo two years of rigorous training. Studies included tropical hygiene, tropical products, accounting, criminal law, map making and map reading, ethnology, details of native labor and native administration, and the general duties of patrol officers.

To qualify for appointment each candidate was supposed to have passed either his intermediate or final high school examinations. In the 1920s most Australian schoolchildren terminated their education in the third, or intermediate, year of high school at about the age of fourteen or fifteen. A few, however, continued on through the entire five-year program, especially if planning to attend a university. Upon completion of training a cadet was to spend another year at the University of Sydney studying anthropology, practical geography, and hygiene.

According to H. R. Niall of Lae, one of the young men appointed in 1927, Errol was given a temporary appointment pending confirmation of his references in Sydney. Six youths had won these coveted posts, but for some reason one of them failed to appear. Errol took his place and was assigned to Kokopo which, known as Herbertshöhe, had once served as capital of German New Guinea. The *Rabaul Times* reports he was soon competing in a tennis tournament at the local club and participating in swimming meets as well. Within six weeks, however, the *Montoro* returned with letters from Dalgety and Company Limited, and Errol's brief career as a cadet patrol officer came to an end.

At this juncture in the unfolding Flynn saga one must compare British and American editions of *My Wicked, Wicked Ways*. Some six pages of what Errol wrote concerning these cadet days did not reach the eyes of most readers within the Empire. Those who did see this sequence, especially old time New Guinea residents, were furious and raised such a hullabaloo that two hundred and twenty-seven lines were deleted from the original version published by G. P. Putnam's Sons of New York City.

What stirred local hackles was Cadet Flynn's description of an expedition he said he made to punish natives who had massacred four prospectors near Madang on New Guinea's northern coast. After an exciting (even thrilling) passage across the Bismarck Sea from Rabaul, Flynn says he led his little group of native police boys into the steaming jungle. Two weeks later they rendezvoused at the scene of the tragedy with a district officer and several other patrols.

In short order a group of suspects was rounded up, gallows constructed, and those found guilty summarily dispatched before a throng of excited natives. While these executions were supposed to demonstrate the severity of white man's justice and teach onlookers a lesson, Errol tells how each dangling body—especially if a condemned individual struggled in a grotesque fashion—provoked shouts, festive laughter, and widespread applause. Flynn says he had difficulty "holding his guts" as he watched these macabre proceedings and was delighted when the day finally ended.

While events obviously did not take place as described, Errol Flynn's tale has some basis in fact. He apparently was inspired by the famous "Nakani Massacre" which occurred in the Talasea District of New Britain. Four Australian prospectors were slaughtered there in October of 1926, a year before our provisional cadet arrived in the islands. Although some readers of *My Wicked, Wicked Ways* protested that natives *never* were hanged, issues of the official *New Guinea Gazette* tell a different story. Even Flynn's description of hilarity at a hanging is hardly original; however, it is most unlikely that youngsters in training near Rabaul on New Britain would ever have been sent on patrol in New Guinea several hundred miles away.

J. K. McCarthy's *Patrol Into Yesterday: My New Guinea Years* (Melbourne, 1963) gives a thorough and undoubtedly much more accurate account of the Nakani (or Nakanai) Massacre. McCarthy says the four men were slain at the village of Silanga about one hundred and fifty miles southwest of Rabaul as the result of very questionable acts (seizure of two women, rape of another, and theft of a pig) by a native constable attached to a government patrol. These provocations so enraged the villagers that, when a party of prospectors appeared a fortnight later, they fell upon them with disastrous results. Four whites and three natives were killed, and two other natives wounded. The villagers, according to McCarthy, probably thought the group was another patrol; and, when they failed to see the hated constable, they withdrew and permitted two survivors and their bearers to escape.

News of these deaths stirred an immediate reaction in Rabaul and set into motion a horrifying sequence of events. The administration, only five years old and unsure of itself, bowed to public pressure and organized a semi-official posse to apprehend the killers. Some fifty white residents, deputized as special aides, set out with nearly a hundred policemen, a horde of native prisoners temporarily re-released from the local jail to serve as porters, and a small arsenal of firearms, including a rusty Maxim machine gun.

In the midst of this uproar an opportunistic plantation owner decided it would be a fine time to recruit laborers who (he thought) would be very eager to leave the area. He was dead wrong. They much preferred the unfolding drama and impending excitement and refused to budge. Angered, the white man burned down a village almost under the very noses of a half dozen important government officials. He was immediately arrested and shipped back to Rabaul.

After this comic opera diversion, the ponderous, improvised force started the rough trek inland to Silanga, seven miles from the coast. They found the village deserted and set up camp at nearby Umu. There they were attacked by a great number of natives; but, warned by the bark of a dog, they easily repulsed the onslaught. Twenty-three spear-waving warriors were killed without any loss to the make-shift army.

McCarthy comments rather testily that the elated volunteers now felt their excursion to be a rousing success and sailed back to Rabaul in triumph. They set out to teach the damned Nakani a lesson and had done so; but, speaking as a government employee, he was thoroughly disgusted with the outcome. The wayward constable was still at large; those guilty of murdering the prospectors had not been captured; the region was quite naturally in an uproar; and it would take months of cautious diplomacy to re-establish any rapport with the native population. District Officer Edward Taylor (the same man Flynn tells us led the New Guinea expedition in which he participated) set up a patrol post at Malutu and began the onerous task of repairing the damage of recent weeks. Meanwhile, other officials hunted down sixteen natives who were taken to Rabaul for trial. These men were convicted and sentenced to death for killing the four prospectors, but subsequently they were given fifteen-year sentences instead. McCarthy, who witnessed these legal proceedings, found himself assigned to the troubled Malutu post a short time after the trials ended.

While this massacre occurred twelve months before Flynn arrived in Rabaul, the expeditionary force and the courtroom drama were still a ready topic of conversation in October of 1927, the most exciting thing that had happened in New Britain since World War I ended.

After Errol was dismissed from government service, Niall recalls that he became assistant manager of Kenabot Plantation a few miles southwest osf Kokopo. This position was followed by a series of jobs including a stint at the Adams-Cooper Garage and Service Station in Rabaul. Niall says he next went to Kavieng in New Ireland as manager of Lemus Plantation. In his autobiography Flynn fails to mention either Kenabot or his career as a grease monkey, but does tell us about New Ireland, although he writes that he went to "Matinalawa" Plantation and includes, naturally enough, a potpourri of South Seas erotica.

Matanalawa (sometimes spelled Matanalaua) is on the north coast of New Hanover, about fifty miles from Kavieng, chief port of New Ireland. New Hanover, a sizeable island perhaps twenty by forty miles in area, lies west of the northern end of New Ireland. The sea between, a distance of twenty-five miles, is awash with tiny bits of land. One of these specks is Lemus Island. Coconuts and copra are the principal products of these islands, although Flynn's proud boast that at "Matinalawa" he was the only white man within fifty miles seems a bit exaggerated.

Sometime in 1928 Errol became ill (perhaps from malaria), returned to Rabaul, and from there embarked upon another haphazard round of jobs. Chronological sequence is vague indeed, but it appears that during the next eighteen months or so he was employed on several plantations, worked briefly as an air cargo clerk, and roved as a recruiter of native labor aboard a schooner plying the dark rivers of New Guinea's north coast. At times, he was out of work; but, jaunty as ever in well-worn shorts, white undershirt, dirty tennis shoes, and an ever-present little silver charm on a chain about his neck, he could often be found in local pubs, although there is no evidence he was then a heavy drinker. Some contemporaries say the reverse was true. He was more interested in keeping a clear head for poker, an occasional punch-up, or a bedroom adventure.

The tropical barroom of those days was obviously more than a mere water hole. Set in communities which might lack nearly all of the facilities common to carefully developed villages and towns, it was social centre, employment agency, psuedo bank and loan office, contact point—a crossroads of information and opportunity where any young man, even if temporarily insolvent, had to be. Errol, a slim six-foot-two, was a commanding figure in a crowd of drinkers anywhere. Some individuals who knew him in the islands said he was simply the sort of person whose mere presence created an aura of excitement. Wherever he was things seemed to happen. Young, dynamic, confident, swift with his fists, and adept at cards, he appeared to be a man among men . . . and women, too! If he jumped from job to job with amazing dexterity his career undoubtedly mirrored those of scores of other men swilling warm beer at his side. Yet, the reputation of "rover" was admittedly somewhat risky.

The story of the gold strike which lured Errol Flynn to the island of New Guinea can be summed up rather quickly. For two decades prior to World War I assorted Germans, Australians, and British roamed over the island in search of instant wealth without much success. Then, in the early 1920s "Shark-Eye" Bill Park found rich alluvial deposits in the rivers and streams of the Wau-Bulolo area, especially Edie Creek. Soon, aided by five associates, the so-called "Big Six" began to exploit their find. Others followed and between 1924 and 1928 the annual output of the previous metal rose from 7,417 to 113,874 ounces. With gold selling at about six dollars an ounce this was obviously a lucrative enterprise, although in cold cash copra remained by far the mandate's most valuable export throughout the 1920s.

In 1930 gold production began to decline, but this downward trend proved temporary. The introduction of giant dredges, flown up piece by piece and assembled at the fields, and skillful utilization of air transport stimulated an even greater boom. In the decade from 1921 to 1931 New Guinea exported 403,703 ounces of gold. During a twelve-month period (June 1931-June 1932) the total extracted was slightly more than one-fourth of that amount—108,647 ounces—and the following year a whopping 196,823 ounces of gold was shipped to the outside world. However, it is apparent this was no longer a game little boys could play. Air transport, monster machines, and spiraling labor costs eliminated all but a few large syndicates and pathetic hopefuls who hung on with faith and tenacity.

Bert Weston, who, like many young Australians, went to seek his fortune in the islands, recalls the New Guinea he knew in the 1920s. Weston soon abandoned mining under convincing pressure exerted by hostile native arrows and reverted to his natural occupation of construction. He became chief engineer of the airfield at Lae, a community of eighteen whites and a swarm of natives when he first arrived, and remained there until 1940.

> It was a rough-and-tumble crowd in those days. Very few of those hard-bitten men could write, in a literary sense. There was no religion, no politics, no trade unions. You got along on what other people thought of you. If you didn't measure up you had to get out.

In the early or mid-1920s, lacking wharfs and facilities of any kind, men were literally dumped on the ishtmus at Salamaua, gateway to the Morobe fields some twenty miles down the coast from Lae. Lae, lying on the north bank of the Markham River, thanks to the efforts of men like Weston, became the air terminus of the gold traffic from the highlands. Today it is a thriving community of fifteen to twenty thousand souls while Salamaua, blasted out of existence by World War II, can boast only a few holiday homes owned by successful Lae businessmen.

As soon as a would-be miner's water-soaked gear was stored safely in a native hut, he headed for Salamaua's lone pub where, over beers (2/6 or thirty cents a bottle, whiskey 1/- per drink), he learned the hard facts of his new life. At Wau, by the way, beer was 6/3 or seventy-five cents a bottle. Often the neophyte would meet a bloke who had taken out a miner's right for £1 and staked a claim. Claims had to be worked within a year or forfeited. As suds flowed it was not difficult to come to some sort of agreement: you go up there and develop that claim of mine and we'll go fifty-fifty on costs and returns. As for financing, Burns Philp and Carpenter were willing to back almost anyone with potential for hard work. Sometimes men returned on stretchers, riddled with disease and tropical ulcers . . . sometimes not at all. Few came back richer. Like most gold strikes, those in first and hangers-on—suppliers, shippers, pub-keepers, etc.—were the real winners.

Mrs. Allen Innes, who ran a fine hotel at Salamaua from the late 1920s to the mid 1930s, says her establishment was often more hospital than hotel. Frequently she had as many as 160 at meals. Much of the time, however, she was fussing over miners suffering from malnutrition and tropical disorders and travelers who often contracted malaria and dysentery. Fortunately she was a professional nurse, having served in the Fiji Islands during World War I where she briefly ministered to the needs of Count Felix von Luckner, commander of the raider, *Seeadler*, when he was taken prisoner.

Her husband, a large, rugged man, was also deeply involved in the gold fields saga, although not a miner himself. As merchandise manager for Burns Philp at Rabaul he was instrumental in advancing supplies to the "Big Six" when their luck had nearly run out. As soon as gold was discovered and hundreds began to flock to the Morobe District, Innes quit Burns Philp and joined up with the fledgling Salamaua Trading Company. By 1935 this complex included a large bustling store crammed with a myriad of goods, an ice-making plant, and the hotel.

Despite heat and disease, life in the Salamaua-Lae area had its lighter moments. The Inneses, Westons, and scores of other ex-New Guinea residents now retired to Sydney and Queensland's Gold Coast remember with great pleasure the good times of those days.

There was no depression up there during those years. It was an exciting place to live in and a good time to be alive. We were young and there were picnics and cruises on weekends, dancing and parties at the hotel. Perhaps the only pain was when our children, tots of six or so, had to go all the way to Australia to attend school. The separation hurt. It really hurt.

After 1928 steamers called at Salamaua every six weeks and residents flocked aboard to gorge themselves on fresh food and inexpensive grog—delighted to be free for a few days from rancid butter and tinned meat. Then, within a short time, they returned to the normal diet of hornbill soup, pigeon rissole, New Zealand canned meat, sweet potatoes (with the leaves stewed as vegetables), tinned apricots, and bread of a sort concocted from homemade yeast. Between ship visits, according to Weston, men at Lae occasionally blew off steam by holding impromptu shirt-ripping nights at the pub, and on Sundays one might be fortunate enough to get a good dinner at a Lutheran Mission nearby.

Bert Weston and his wife remember seeing Errol Flynn from time to time, one of numerous youngsters both propelled from Australia by hard times and drawn northward by the lure of gold. They accepted him as just another bit of flotsam distinguished only by good looks and a huge Alsatian dog, his constant companion. In contrast to many who lived in the islands during those days, Mrs. Weston says she found Errol "a quite pleasant young chap . . . and he didn't owe me any money either"! Others speak less fondly of Errol, undoubtedly because he was a disturbing influence in any small frontier community whose leaders believed devoutly in hard work and the Protestant ethic. Flynn, with his footloose charm and easy morals, was the antithesis of all they stood for. "He was", as one contemporary commented, "what is now called a hippie and the then white population of New Guinea were cubes in outlook, though not necessarily in deed!"

A less friendly portrait of Errol appeared in an Australian journal, *Quadrant* (Spring, 1961), shortly after *My Wicked, Wicked Ways* was published. Eric Feldt obviously was infuriated by some of the tales spun out on its pages. Author of *The Coast Watchers*, a highly readable account of World War II espionage, Feldt attacks much of what Flynn wrote as lies, "all lies". He was district officer at Salamaua when the young roustabout arrived from Gizarum Plantation on Umboi Island at the western end of New Britain where he had been working for a short time. Umboi on Rooke Island is some twenty miles from New Britain and about forty miles from northern New Guinea.

> Soon after his arrival, A. S. Cross, manager of Guinea Airways, told me while I was at Lae that he was looking for a man to manage their branch at Wau where his job would be mainly to receive and distribute the cargo flown in, and did I know anyone who could do it? I replied that there was a likely looking young man at Salamaua named Flynn, and soon afterwards Flynn was given the job and flown to Wau. Flown in—he did not walk as he so graphically describes in his book.

Feldt says Errol did not last long at Wau, and this may have been as close as he ever got to gold in the late 1920s—sorting and delivering freight consigned to miners. This former colonial official demolishes other stories which, in truth, make the future Hollywood star's autobiography such delightful reading. He states categorically that Flynn was never tried for murder in Salamaua, a tale Errol exploits to the fullest. Had such a trial occurred during those years Feldt himself would have been the presiding magistrate.

H. R. Niall, who as a cadet trainee lived with Flynn at Kokopo, says the young Tasmanian somehow caught the attention of W. A. Money, owner of the Siassi Island Plantations near Umboi. Money was one of the original "Big Six" who began development of the Edie Creek field in the highlands, and Flynn next became a labor recruiter on a schooner which belonged to Money. While the crew's primary task was to probe river villages and nearby jungle for healthy black workers, it appears their vessel also carried cargo and passengers at times. In contrast to his short terms as plantation overseer, garage mechanic, and air cargo clerk, this job, perhaps because it was on the water, seems to have stymied Flynn's wanderlust momentarily. Also, it is possible that, separated for much of the time from pubs, beer, and women he slept better and more frequently.

Among Flynn's companions in this venture was "Dusty" Miller who would become a well-known local entrepreneur in the 1930s and a flyer in Europe during World War II. In May of 1940 he dispatched this radiogram to a startled Winston Churchill, the new resident of 10 Downing Street: "Samarai. May 9. Congratulations: Hold fast. We are coming – Dusty Miller." As a gold fields pub keeper "Dusty" instituted his own unique accounting system which seemed to work well enough. A friend of miners and eager to help them, he drank with the boys each evening and got roaring drunk right along with them. The next morning, with heavy head, he and a native assistant would tally up the damage: how much beer, whiskey, and gin had disappeared. Then he would weigh this total against a roster of the miners who usually bellied up to the bar.

> Bill hasn't been doin' well lately. We won't charge him anything. Mike has had a run of luck, £5. Ed wasn't here, as I recall. No charge. John and Eric drank a bit and are doin' goddamned well. £4 each.

And so it went . . . and rarely did anyone complain.

As labor recruiters Flynn and Miller were individuals of some importance in the strange primitive economy which was developing in New Guinea at the close of the 1920s. In fact, the skill of a recruiter could determine success or failure for the entire gold-mining industry. Without the aid of hundreds of black hands and thousands of sweaty muscles little if any yellow metal would have reached the coast. That this recruiting often bordered upon slavery is widely recognized. Flynn even spoke of himself as a "blackbirder" or "slaver" while chatting with a startled Hollywood reporter a decade or so later.

Yet, in fairness to the Australian government, its harassed representatives tried valiantly to regulate recruitment procedures. Each recruiter was licensed, labor contracts were executed at the nearest district office, and a native had to undergo medical examination. If sound of body, limb, and wind (a minimum chest expansion of thirty-one inches), then a recruit might sign up for a term of one, two, or three years. The recruiter usually got £5 per boy per year accordingly. The employer had to supply each worker with a storage box, blanket, enamel bowl, and spoon. Hours of work, salary, and medical treatment were specified by law, and employers were responsible for getting their boys back home when contracts expired.

Even what a native ate was clearly spelled out in government bulletins. Each day he was to receive one pound of rice, one-half pound of barley or wheat, one-quarter pound of dried beans, peas, or lentils, and four ounces of fresh meat—or one and one-half pounds of preserved meat or fish weekly. He was also supposed to get sugar, tea, salt, and one and one-half pounds of biscuits per week.

An article in the *Rabaul Times* (29 October, 1926) stressed the problems facing anyone who wished to get to the gold fields. The hard trek up into the highlands above Salamaua took at least seven days; and, although one covered only about fifty to sixty air miles, he traveled several hundred miles up and down. The potential miner faced dysentery, typhoid, blackwater fever, and native arrows. The nearest point of entry from the outside world was Rabaul. The fare to that port from Sydney or Brisbane was £18 and £1 per day maintenance while aboard ship at Rabaul. Passage from Rabaul to Salamaua cost Europeans £6, natives 25/-.

The *Times* cautioned that a miner needed a grub stake of at least £1,000. He had to produce £100 in cash at government headquarters and deposit £50 to cover possible fines, return fare, etc. It would cost, according to this weekly, another £700 to maintain two men and fifteen boys at the fields for six months.

> The best boys are from the hill country behind Finschhafen Lutheran Mission, the hilly reaches of the Markham River, and other mountainous areas of the Morobe District itself.

The annual report which the Australian government submitted to the League of Nations (1926-7) also sheds light upon how mining was developing on the eve of Errol Flynn's arrival in the islands and helps to explain why he and scores like him found it almost impossible to become successful miners.

> Prospecting in the Territory is extremely difficult owing to the ruggedness of the country and to the fact that the surface is covered by timber and a network of roots. Until a depot for stores is established on the field, it is not possible for prospectors to travel far in the examination of new country.

> Mining operations are hampered considerably by the difficulties of transportation and the rough nature of the country to be traversed. In the initial stages of the Bulolo gold-field, all tools and stores had to be carried from the beach at Salamaua over steep mountains, for a distance of about 65 miles. As the maximum load that a native is permitted to carry is restricted to 50 lbs., it is impossible for heavy machinery to be transported to the field.

> A certain measure of relief has resulted from the use of aeroplanes, but the number of such machines employed will need to be increased if the requirements of the mining community are to be provided for by means of aerial transport.

Two roads from the coast to the field are now being constructed by the Administration, but it is anticipated that a period of twelve months will probably elapse before they become available for wheeled traffic.

A whole brace of twelve months would go by before trucks and cars drove up the steep hills toward Wau. War alone provided even a rudimentary track inland. Perhaps it should be noted that, at least in the 1920s, all food had to be transported to the highlands. This meant that of the fifty pounds a native carried twenty might be his own rations. In addition, boss boys had to keep a sharp eye on carriers who often tried to "lighten" their loads *en route*.

In August of 1929 the Sydney *Sun* featured a thorough-going account of life at the gold fields and in Salamaua. The writer emphasized all good land at Edie Creek had been pegged, and it was hard living and hard working up in that cold, wet climate 7,000 feet above sea level. A fifty-pound mat of rice which cost 11/- at Salamaua sold for 48/- at Wau, and other costs escalated accordingly. Yet Salamaua was an almost unbelievable round of hard-drinking gaiety. "No one," wrote this reporter, "takes life seriously." Champagne before breakfast was not unknown, although wine sold for 30/- per bottle and a brandy and soda cost as much as a bottle of beer, 2/6. Even funerals could be hilarious occasions. He told of one mourner showing up in dressing gown, bottle of beer in pocket, and a bunch of white flowers in hand. "Bill", he was informed "would have liked it that way."

This reporter also told his readers of an episode which one suspects may well describe our hero in a less than heroic moment. After all, although the protagonist is not identified, there could not have been many recruiters of those days accompanied by a large dog.

A youthful recruiter invited an old, grey-haired miner 'outside' to finish an argument, but they had hardly left the bar before the recruiter re-entered it head first—the old man had given him 'the flying mare'. That settled the argument, but later the recruiter, egged on by others in search of fun, remarked, 'Well, if I can't beat him, my dog can!' and promptly set the animal on the old man. But the latter, quite undaunted, seized the dog by the scruff of the neck, swung him around, knocked its owner into the street on the second swing, and threw his dog after him.

Errol's months on Money's schooner appears to form the basis of many episodes found in his autobiographical novel published in 1946 and in the novelistic autobiography which appeared soon after his death. In both he tells of life aboard the *Maski* which cruised New Guinea waters carrying cargo from port to port. (Roughly translated, "maski" means "it doesn't matter".) The *Maski* is not cited in any shipping lists found in the *Rabaul Times* of those years, although the *Matupi*, another ship on which Flynn claims to have worked, did exist . . . however, its skipper was a man named Boles, not Ed Bowen as related by Errol.

The most perplexing of these stories concerns a trip up the Sepik with an American movie crew. Expanded and much embellished it became the principal theme of the novel, *Showdown*. Dr. Herman F. Erben, a tropical disease specialist, explorer, and amateur movie maker, presumably hired Flynn to make this expedition so he could shoot a documentary on head-hunters. Somehow Erben becomes "Joel Swartz" in both *Showdown* and *My Wicked, Wicked Ways*, and in the latter he also takes on yet a third name, "Dr. Gerrit H. Koets". Tony Thomas, Rudy Behlmer, and Clifford McCarty wrestled with this phenomenon in their fine compendium, *The Films of Errol Flynn* (New York, 1969), but found few answers.

Errol even credits "Swartz" with providing the break which got him his first movie role in October of 1932, but there is substantial evidence in the Sydney area to prove this assertion pure fancy. Nevertheless, several individuals who knew Flynn during these years (among them Mrs. Lillian Barclay Miller, widow of "Dusty", better known as "Tiger Lil") confirm the fact that he was involved with a movie making venture of some sort along the New Guinea coast circa 1929-30.

While apparently changing Erben's name to Swartz, Errol often uses real names in his novel while altering those same names somewhat in his autobiography. One example of this strange, inexplicable confusion is Ah Chee, a well-known hotel keeper of Rabaul. He is correctly identified in *Showdown* but becomes "Ah Sim" or merely "Sim" in *My Wicked, Wicked Ways*. Ah Chee, who died late in 1933 much lamented, ran Chee's Iour Gnee Hotel:

> Home of travelers and tourists—superior accommodations—reasonable charges—wines and spirits true to label—motor garage—cars for hire.

In October of 1929 Errol was back in Rabaul, probably staying in Ah Chee's "superior accommodations". Once more he was sick and evidently had had his fill of recruiting. On the 22nd he boarded the *Montoro* bound for Sydney, arriving there on the 30th. If one can believe *My Wicked, Wicked Ways*, this trip was prompted by a bad case of gonorrhea acquired from a Kavieng lovely. Decision to flee southward was made more urgent by clumsy self-inflicted treatment which sounds much, much worse than the disease itself!

Only with a loan of £100 from his old pal "Dusty" could Errol even contemplate such a journey. However, on the eve of his departure Flynn tells us he got into a poker game and walked away with a small fortune of £400. Ill and certainly very uncomfortable, but richer in both coin and experience, Errol Leslie Thomson Flynn, age twenty years, four months, and ten days, arrived back in Sydney. Slightly more than two years had elapsed since he first sailed out through the Heads for the tropics. New Guinea "phase one" was at an end.

# Chapter Three

## The Cruise
of the *Sirocco*, 1930

Errol remained in Sydney for about six months, regaining his health while at the same time savoring the joys of metropolitan life. During these weeks he resumed his associations with Ken Hunter-Kerr, the Dibbs girls and their set, and established a romantic rapport with Naomi which eventually would lead to a formal engagement. Sometime early in 1930 Flynn happened upon an old yacht in a shipyard located in Neutral Bay on the north shore of Sydney's magnificent harbor. The *Sirocco* solidly built of ironbark and kauri, was nearly fifty years old. It had recently changed hands several times, but this was love at first sight and perhaps the most enduring and least tempestuous of Errol's many affairs.

Once master of the *Sirocco* never again would he be far from deck and sea. In fact, at the time of his death in 1959 the aging star had gone to Vancouver to negotiate the sale of the *Zaca*, a successor to the old, weather-beaten *Sirocco*. In mid-March of 1930, accompanied by three friends, he sailed out through the Heads bound for New Guinea. This cruise proved more adventurous than anticipated (it lasted nearly six months instead of the projected six weeks) but was less hair-raising than the tale told in *Beam Ends* seven years later.

Several sources tell us much about how Errol spent his sojourn in Australia's largest city—*My Wicked, Wicked Ways, Beam Ends*, and recollections of those who knew Flynn during these months. The autobiography devotes only a few paragraphs to this period. Errol says he slowly recovered from his bout with gonorrhea, drifted around town in an aimless fashion, ran out of coin, and worked for a brief time as a "bottle smeller". His task was to sniff soft drink bottles to determine if they had been filled with kerosene, turpentine, or other noxious liquids. During these weeks of separating "good" from "bad" bottles, in his leisure moments Flynn haunted the bar at Usher's Hotel, a well-known landmark much favored by the New Guinea crowd when in town. One day a barmaid told him an English syndicate wanted to buy his Edie Creek claim which lay between two leases the company already owned. Errol immediately sold out for £2,000; and, when the haze of celebration cleared, he discovered he had paid £1,500 for a yacht named *Sirocco*. Unable to dispose of the hulk, he decided to sail the craft back to New Guinea.

*Beam Ends* relates a somewhat different story. It opens with Errol and one of his pals, Trelawney Adams, on board the *Baltimore* in Adelaide. They had shipped on in Sydney as ordinary seamen, but found living and working conditions intolerable. At Albany, a port in Western Australia, they finally jumped ship and made their way back to Sydney. There Errol began sniffing bottles learned of his Edie Creek windfall, sold out for a mere £1,000, and woke up the next morning with the yacht, a devastating hangover, and only £200 in cash. "It will always be something of a mystery to me", he wrote, "how I came to acquire the yacht, *Sirocco*."

Those who knew Flynn, newspaper files, and other related sources paint yet another picture. Issues of Sydney's *Daily Commercial News & Shipping List* fail to mention a vessel named the *Baltimore* during these months, so we can assume the trip to Adelaide and points west probably never took place. It is equally unlikely that Errol held title to any claim at Edie Creek in 1930. Even if he did, a company seeking his land only had to wait a few more months; and, if not worked, it could acquire the property from local authorities for much, much less. Paying out several thousand pounds makes little sense. In addition, at that time Errol told Ken Hunter-Kerr he got the money for the *Sirocco* from Burns Philp. He said the territorial administration had approved establishment of a small store in a remote district of New Guinea. He got there first, set up a rudimentary trading post, and Burns Philp bought him out.

The truth is there was no windfall, no claim, no trading post. During these months Errol worked at several casual jobs. H. R. Niall, his fellow cadet at Kokopo, met Flynn on a Sydney street early in 1930. Errol said he was earning his living by modeling suits for R. C. Hagon Limited. Photographs of his handsome, well-tailored physique were being flashed daily upon scores of movie screens as part of a dreary advertising parade which still both bores and amuses Australian theater-goers. R. C. Hagon Limited, no longer in existence, was located at 129 King Street, an address which now houses the Tasmanian Government Tourist Bureau.

At about the time Niall encountered him, Flynn the model was becoming obsessed with the prospects of buying a yacht owned by Lars Halvorsen, a Norwegian-born boat builder who had come to Sydney via South Africa. The *Sirocco* had been constructed by W. M. Ford for Edward William Knox, heir to the Colonial Sugar fortune, in 1881. During the next few years the boat was conspicuous in numerous local races. It took first prize of £30 at the Balmain Regatta on 9 November, 1881, a day marred (according to the *Sydney Morning Herald*) by a luncheon at which no one proposed a toast to the health of His Royal Highness, the Prince of Wales. Two years later the *Sirocco* won an exciting challenge race to Bondi and during the 1883-4 season flew from its masthead the pennant of the Royal Sydney Yacht Club's commodore.

When Commodore Knox withdrew from active competition he continued to sail his ten-ton, cutter-rigged craft—thirty-eight feet, seven inches long with straight stem and deep keel—as a pleasure cruiser. Commenting upon the decision of the Yacht Club's senior member (1869) to sell the *Sirocco*, the *Sydney Morning Herald* said on 23 March, 1927:

Errol as Fletcher Christian, from Charles Chauvel's *In the Wake of the Bounty*, a small book published in Sydney in 1933 to promote the movie by the same name.

*Left:* Professor Flynn, photo made in Ireland in 1930s or 1940s.
*Right:* Errol's mother, photo apparently made in Hobart by J.
W. Beattie, perhaps 1913-1914.

Errol at about age four, photo made in Hobart by J. W. Beattie.

*Above:* Group of friends at Ken Hunter-Kerr's cottage at King's Cross, 1926-27. "Doddie Dog" and Errol in foreground. Left to right, Naomi Dibbs, Cecile Dibbs (third of Dibbs sisters), Phyl McLauchlan (later Lady Collins, wife of Vice-Admiral Sir John Collins, once Austsralian High Commissioner to New Zealand), and Miriam Dibbs in rakish "Eton" cut. The cottage, an old stable, stood on the site of the Motel King's Cross.
*Below: Sirocco*, from *Sydney Morning Herald*, 22 March 1927.

A party at a polo match at Kensington Race Course (Sydney) now the campus of the University of New South Wales, 1926-27. Errol is 17 and working at Dalgety's. Seated on the ground (left to right) Errol, Ken Hunter-Kerr, Miriam Dibbs, Naomi Dibbs. Behind, Enid Hussey Cooper, Edward Ashley Cooper (Enid's brother and the actor, Ashley Cooper), and Nina Throsby, owner of Throsby Park, historic home near Moss Vale, N.S.W.

Errol, age 20, back in Sydney after two years in the islands, late 1929. Photo by local society photographer . . . dated in lower right corner.

*Left:* Naomi Dibbs, engagement photo which appeared in the *Daily Pictorial*, 26 January 1931.

*Right:* Errol on the deck of the *Sirocco* at Halvorsen's boatyard in Neutral Bay, N.S.W. He is cradling a hair brush in mock heroics. February/March 1930.

*Above:* Errol at Bowral striking traditional "proud owner" pose with car not his (probably a Morris or a Standard), early 1931.

*Below:* Errol and friends at tea break during tennis afternoon at Nancy Houston's court at Burradoo, N.S.W. near Bowral, home of Naomi Dibbs's parents. Errol and Gradley Ryrie, son of Major General Sir Granville Ryrie, are seated on the ground wearing blazers. Behind them are Ken Hunter-Kerr and Nancy Houston (hostess). Early 1931.

*Above*: Errol's tobacco plantation home near Laloki (1931-32), from the Australian magazine, *People*, 18 January 1961.

*Below*: Sydney beach scene. August/September 1932. Left to right, Miriam and Ken Hunter-Kerr, who were married on 2 January 1932. Errol, and Naomi Dibbs. On this day or during a similar outing Flynn was seen by the casting director of Cinesound Studios. This led to his first movie role

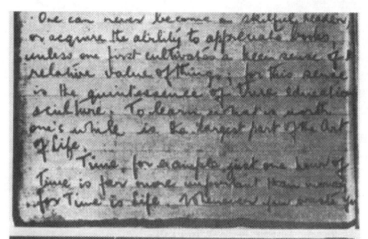

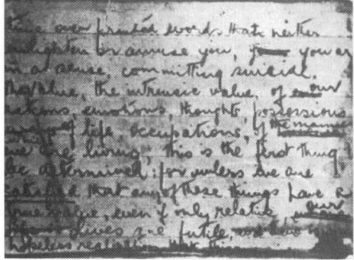

Pages from Errol's notebook found in New Guinea in 1935. Copies from *People*, 18 January 1961. The original notebook has disappeared. Mrs. Innes, who found it, apparently sold it to a New York City autograph dealer in the late 1960s.

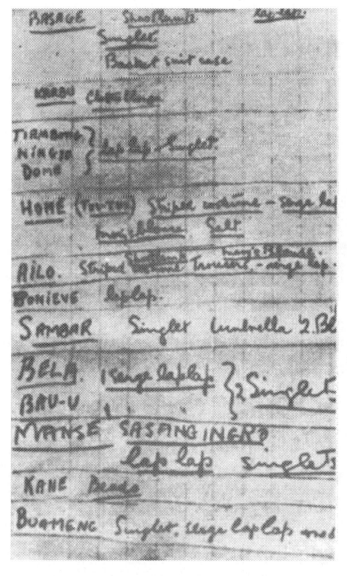

At the back of the notebook Errol listed the workers he had
engaged and the goods he had paid them to sign on.

Publicity photo taken on the yacht *Zaca* by Floyd McCarty of Warner Brothers.

On set in England (1951) with Joanne Dru and fr ends.

Shot from *Captain Blood* (1935). Flynn's first big break in Hollywood.

Photo of *Zaca*, Errol's last yacht, in Jamaica, which appeared on a Christmas card sent to Australian relatives by his parents in the 1950s.

Patrice Wymore and daughter Arnella, probably taken in late 1950s about the time of Flynn's death. Arnella, his fourth child, was born in 1952.

There is not a sailing enthusiast, from the dinghy boys to the yachtsmen, who is not familiar with the sight of the big black yacht which cruises in the vicinity of the races, Saturday after Saturday during the summer, with Mr. Knox at the tiller.

In the late 1920s the craft passed quickly through several hands and underwent some superficial change until acquired by Halvorsen. According to his sons, Bjarne and Harold, Errol and his parents visited their father's shipyard two or three times. Finally Mrs. Flynn wrote a check for £120 and her son became the proud owner of the good ship *Sirocco*.

This act by Lily Mary raises several questions. Errol often reminds us of a well-established fray with his mother. He says they fought continuously, even concluding *My Wicked, Wicked Ways* on this note: "My war with Mother drones on steadily, towards a silent truce." He also reports that his mother told a New York newsman in the 1950s that "Errol was a nasty little boy". It is quite possible this conflict existed and Mrs. Flynn was merely trying to close the breach with a gift which represents a substantial outlay in the depths of the depression. The Halvorsens recall her comment that she wanted her son to settle down and "get into something" . . . a trade, an occupation of some sort.

A Sydney University professor who sailed from London to Melbourne with "Theo" in June of 1931 remembers how very concerned the father was. He, too, felt it was high time Errol began a career. Professor Flynn, by the way, was returning to Hobart to wind up his affairs at the University of Tasmania preparatory to becoming Professor of Zoology at Queen's College in Belfast. He held this position in Northern Ireland until his retirement in 1948. Thus, although mama signed the check, purchase of the *Sirocco* may well have been a joint effort by two troubled (and estranged) parents who were trying to help their wayward, twenty-year-old son find his bearings.

Errol immediately ordered alterations totaling £100, and by mid-February of 1930 the boat was ready for a test run. The Halvorsens received only partial payment for this work and years later tried to collect £45 from Flynn the movie star. Although they were unsuccessful and did not even receive the usual smiling photo, Lars Halvorsen and his youthful client remained the best of friends, for the boat builder was completely captivated by Flynn's roguish charm. After Errol departed for New Guinea they continued to carry on a lighthearted correspondence, Flynn writing to inquire about other projects under construction when he left and relating details of his trip northward along Australia's east coast. Bjarne, then only fourteen years old, concedes he was not at all surprised by Errol's rise to stardom. He recalls seeing the startlingly handsome young man at his father's yard and immediately thinking "he oughta be in pictures . . . I have never seen the like of him before or since". His brother, Harold, says Flynn kept a car at Neutral Bay early in 1930 and often borrowed evening clothes from various acquaintances when going out on the town.

On the afternoon of Saturday, 15 February, Errol and a group of his friends set out on a brief shakedown cruise to test a new Swedish oil engine (a semi-diesel) and other innovations. The party included Ken Hunter-Kerr, Charlie Burt, Trelawney Adams, T. H. Arrowsmith, and a photographer on the staff of Sydney's *Daily Pictorial*. According to a story published in the Monday edition of that newspaper the group planned to go shark fishing outside of the Heads, but were caught up in a violent story. They experienced considerable engine trouble and were blown back into Neutral Bay. A picture taken during less hectic moments shows a broad-shouldered Flynn in undershirt and yachting cap surrounded by Arrowsmith in tam, Hunter-Kerr, and Burt. This article indicates Flynn, Burt, and Adams planned to set out for New Guinea within a few weeks aboard the "Errol", apparently a temporary name for the old *Sirocco*.

Hunter-Kerr says the events of that February afternoon transpired somewhat differently. There was no fishing trip, no storm, but considerable difficulty with the Swedish engine. The group eventually drifted up the coast to Palm Beach, some twenty miles north of Sydney, where they spent the night. *En route* Burt, unaware that Errol had used the coffee pot to prime the reluctant engine, brewed up a fresh supply of java which made everyone (except Hunter-Kerr) seasick. So much for Errol Flynn's unique ability to smell oil and kerosene! The following day the engine was repaired, but continued to cause trouble in the months ahead.

Several weeks later, the precise date is not known, the *Sirocco* slipped out of Sydney bound for New Guinea. The crew, in addition to the skipper and owner, included Adams, Burt, and Rex Long-Innes. H. F. Trelawney Adams, recipient of a mechanical science degree from Cambridge University in 1927, was a native of England with Tasmanian connections. Burt, a short, stocky, rather solemn character from the Isle of Man, like Errol was cast in the rover mould. He had been part owner of the *Sirocco* for a brief time, then worked on an outback sheep station, and now was ready to attempt ocean life once more. Rex was the son of  Reginald Heath Long-Innes, an Oxford-educated judge of the Supreme Court of New South Wales.

As this foursome set out there was probably not a true sailor in the lot. Their nautical knowledge was minimal. Errol writes in *Beam Ends* that Rex, for example, could distinguish one end of the ship from the other, but ask him to name them and he was stumped. He also relates how they made so many ill-fated attempts to get under way that friends and relatives finally stopped coming to see them off. Even Rex's mother, after a second tearful farewell, began to treat the whole affair as a lark. "Goodbye, my darling boy, goodbye. Take good care of yourself now. Goodbye. I suppose you'll be home for a game of bridge tonight?"

On 12 March the Sydney *Sun* featured a lengthy article about the *Sirocco* and its stalwart crew, conceding they knew very little about navigation and were taking a great risk embarking upon a dangerous 3,000-mile voyage. Readers were told that Flynn was returning to his plantation two hundred miles from Rabaul, while his companions were in search of gold and adventure. The *Sun* said no gala champagne supper marked their departure. The four youths simply shook hands with a few friends on shore and disappeared. The *Daily Pictorial* noted on 13 March that the thirteen-ton *Sirocco* had left "a few days ago" for New Guinea.

The £45 owed Halvorsen may be one reason for confusion concerning this sailing date. Ken Hunter-Kerr says the adventurers cruised across Sydney Harbor in a leisurely fashion as if going on a casual outing. They then slept on the floor of his small Double Bay flat and got up before daylight to begin their journey. Flynn notes in *Beam Ends* that they departed in the dead of night "unsung and without farewells". The Halvorsen boys maintain their father was well aware of Errol's plans; but, since he was not yet twenty-one, there was no way oft stopping him. Besides, Lars was so very fond of his gregarious, smooth-talking Tasmanian that he probably never considered taking legal action of any kind.

Except for scattered newspaper comment we must rely upon *Beam Ends* for details of the voyage to New Guinea. Published in 1937 by Cassell in Great Britain and Australia and by Longmans, Green in America, the volume bore this dedication:

> To my wife: Who says she will try to find time to read this book one day and who meanwhile has sportingly bought a copy—a gesture I only hope our friends will follow.

Reviewers generally were favorably impressed with the work. The Melbourne *Argus* (11 September, 1937) found it "an entertaining narrative", while the *New York Times* (28 March 1937) called the tale "a wild one". The *Times* noted that although much of the voyage was spent "in merry exploits at ports of call along the Australian coast, almost every hour at sea was hair raising".

As mentioned earlier, Flynn and his buddies planned to sail to New Guinea in about six weeks, but they encountered numerous delays and did not arrive in Port Moresby until sometime in September. Inexperience, bad weather, an uncooperative engine, and riotous living seem to have caused most of their troubles . . . although, admittedly, they were attempting an unusual feat in a small craft ill-equipped for travel in the open sea.

The most unpleasant part of this journey was from Sydney to Brisbane. During the initial run to Port Stephens, some one hundred miles north of Sydney, the boat was awash in high waves as the four youths battled seasickness and learned to adjust to the rigors of maritime life. From there they proceeded to Coff's Harbor where they spent four days and then moved on to Ballina at the mouth of the Richmond River. (Flynn mistakenly calls this community "Banalla".) Because of continuing bad weather and local diversions Ballina, some 360 miles from Sydney, proved to be the first major port of call. For two weeks the *Sirocco's* crew fished, drank, caroused with two of the town's leading citizens (its river pilot and policeman), played poker, and wenched with local talent. Eventually they moved on to Brisbane for a week-long stopover and more of the same. While in Queensland's capital city Errol says he completely overhauled the pesky engine. It took him twenty-four hours to strip it down and twice as long to put it back together again.

By this time, having been at sea for a month, the hardy foursome had acquired some nautical know-how, and life was assuming a routine of sorts. Errol, of course, was captain. Charlie Burt and Trelawney Adams (who had taken on the nickname of "Dook") were the more serious members of the group, while Rex Long-Innes appears to have been almost his skipper's equal as a "con artist". He was a remarkably successful dealer at cards, knew how to charm a well-cooked leg of lamb out of an infatuated barmaid, and seems to have possessed elements of the same smooth, devil-may-care charm which was becoming a Flynn trademark.

These four young men lived by their wits much of the time, often receiving gifts of food and drink from coastal residents delighted with the diversion such visits brought into humdrum lives. Errol concedes their income came from various sources. He and his companions occasionally sold fish they caught, took groups on pleasure cruises, won money playing poker, and during the voyage both he and "Dook" received relatively large sums (£50 or more) from their families. Writing in the mid-thirties Errol says his parents were living in Ireland at the time of this cruise. While untrue, it does fit into the Gaelic background Warner Brothers was trying to construct; and, admittedly, the Flynn's did move to Belfast a year later in 1931.

From Brisbane north the voyage was much more enjoyable. The weather was warmer, and the adventurous crew happened to arrive in two communities—Bundaberg and Rockhampton—just in time to participate to the fullest in the riotous revelry of annual fairs and carnivals. The week in Bundaberg was enlivened by a rodeo, a regatta, and Errol's ten-round match with a Queensland roughneck. He emerged battered, but £5 richer. Actually the *Sirocco* could have sailed from Bundaberg seventy-two hours earlier than it did except for a torrid affair Rex initiated with a local barmaid. Flynn says there was no alternative except to relax, wait, and pray for speedy success. Early in the cruise the four youths, with the chaste "Dock" dissenting, had established two unwritten laws: (1) All affairs of the heart must take precedence over more mundane considerations and be given full opportunity to mature and flower; and (2) Any crew member could have the ship to the exclusion of all others in order to promote this maturation, flowering, de-flowering or whatever one wishes to call it. However, after Rex kept the rest of the group shivering on a cold, rainy wharf for three hours one night, unwritten law number two was summarily repealed.

On the trip from Bundaberg to Rockhampton the *Sirocco* stopped briefly at Gladstone, then a small fishing village but now a centre of growing commercial importance. North of Gladstone the crew decided to attempt the "Narrows", a short cut passage to the Fitzroy River and Rockhampton. However, they ran into trouble and spent hours stuck in mud banks playing poker. Eventually they were rescued by the tide, proceeded to the tiny community of Port Alma, but immediately pushed on to Rockhampton, a city which Rex vowed had an abundant supply of amiable females.

Shortly after the *Sirocco* tied up in that city a local reporter came aboard to interview the four sailors. In *Beam Ends* Flynn identifies the journalist as "Johnson" of the "Rockhampton Graphic". The "Graphic" and much of the material in the article which follows—reproduced from Rockhampton's *Morning Bulletin* (18 June 1930)—are fictional, although Johnson may well have been the name of the man who write these words.

## OFF TO NEW GUINEA

———

## FOUR ADVENTURERS

———

# THE SIROCCO CALLS IN

———

## ONE TIME CRACK YACHT

Long, narrow-waisted, black-hulled, with towering stick showing above the wharf decking, but bearing little signs of the buffeting she has received on her voyage, the *Sirocco* late of the Royal Sydney Yacht Club, now bound for New Guinea and the bêche-de-mer and trochus shell [trade], nine days up from Sydney, lies at the old town wharf.

Fifty years old, but as staunch as the day she slipped into the water for the first time at Circular Quad slips, the *Sirocco* will know a different atmosphere now from the one she has been accustomed to so long. Her youthful crew know where they are going. First there is Captain Errol Flynn, late Cambridge undergrad, now planter on a lonely island 40 miles from mysterious Madang, the island of the 'White Kanakas', where he dispenses high and low justice to his 40 odd natives and bears his share of the white man's burden.

This is our navigator, said Captain Errol Flynn from under his blankets when a *Bulletin* man stepped aboard. 'You'll have to excuse me. Just a touch of malaria. But meet the crew.'

Mr. T. Adams, another young Englishman, is the navigator. Close clipped moustache, accent, and physique brand him unmistakably the product of University. Mr. C. Burt, another member of the crew, is also an Englishman, and Australia is represented by Mr. Rex Long-Innes, son of Judge Long-Innes, who is going forth with the others to seek his fortune in the South Seas.

When they talked it was mostly about their argosy. 'She's old, but she's good,' says the skipper, with pride in his voice, and he told the *Bulletin* man how she logged 14 [knots] for three hours in a howling south-easter that piled them up in Coff's Harbour with a foot of water in the cabin.

'Forty-four feet over all, with a Swedish oil engine, we're not worrying about the weather,' he said.

Already they have had their share of adventure on the trip. They made their names and took their baptisms when they crossed the bars in northern New South Wales in howling gales. They went ashore in Great Sandy Straits and had more than their share of rough weather, but builders builded well 50 years ago, and lean-waisted as she is the *Sirocco* has ten tons of lead under her keel.

In the cabin, where the captain lies with malaria, where the 'crew' sit round in shorts, and where two business-like rifles are fast on clips above the bunks, one might have thought yesterday that the *Sirocco* had reached her destination, for she breathes an atmosphere of romance all too scarce in days when young men no longer go to sea to seek their fortunes.

Errol, who actually may have been suffering from a recurrence of malaria, was soon on his feet again, and when the Rockhampton Carnival opened forty-eight hours later the traveling quartet was in the forefront of the fun. This yearly outburst, a mix of horse racing, stock shows, sports events, dancing, and sideshows, brought thousands of merrymakers to central Queensland's commercial crossroads, a city which also would host many American GIs during World War II. Flynn's first act, however, was to wire Sydney and demand immediate service for the Swedish oil engine so roundly praised in the *Morning Bulletin* interview. But, business completed, he and his pals went about dating local nurses and cavorting with some of the same circus performers they had met during the Bundaberg spree a few days earlier.

On their yacht they entertained chorus girls from the T. C. Williamson troupe which was performing *The Girl Friend, Hold Everything*, and *Sally* at the Wintergarden Theatre. In turn, they were guests in several prominent households (thanks to the social connections of Rex Long-Innes). But most of the time during these three weeks in Rockhampton seems to have been spent in an alcoholic haze shared by Johnson and another sidekick from the journalistic fraternity.

These escapades, which eventually landed Flynn behind bars, are remembered quite clearly by a handful of older residents. Early in 1971 as I sipped beer in the serenity of the Rockhampton Club with George Westacott, a distinguished newspaperman now in his eighties, I asked if he recalled Errol's visit in 1930. "Oh, my yes!" he replied. Then, leaning forward and lowering his voice discreetly, Westacott added, "He and his friends were almost—if you know what I mean, Dr. Moore—*larrikins*!" But, "larrikins" or not, the Rockhampton Public Library obviously is impressed by their exploits for it has not one, but *three* copies of *My Wicked, Wicked Ways* on its shelves.

Errol's 1959 account of these weeks in Rockhampton differs considerably from the 1937 version. In *Beam Ends* he regales readers with hilarious drinking bouts with news reporters and sideshow performers. Then, after forty-eight hours in jail and desperate for money, he tells how he suddenly remembered thirty ounces of gold dust he had deposited to his bank account back in New Guinea some months earlier. A wire to the north brought an unexpected £30. This bonanza was followed almost immediately by another £50, a birthday present from his father "in Ireland".

Delirious with joy at the sight of a small fortune which ensured they would get to New Guinea in style, Flynn almost blew the whole wad in a disastrous roulette game. A police raid ended play, and only with the assistance of Johnson was Errol able to recoup his losses . . . although under circumstances he did not completely understand. While they were being arraigned at police headquarters the newsman told him to make a run for it. Flynn dove for the door, but on the way spied the confiscated money and seized his share. A few minutes later he jumped aboard the *Sirocco*, woke up the rest of the crew, and got under way as quickly as possible.

*My Wicked, Wicked Ways* features a letter written by Errol to his father in Tasmania. It was mailed from Townsville, a port of call north of Rockhampton, and is dated 27 July, 1930. In this report to "Dear Pater" he says nothing about gold dust or birthday presents from Ireland, but describes how addition of a fifth member to the crew, a well-heeled individual, has solved their financial problems. The remainder of this epistle repeats some of the details found in *Beam Ends*—long hazy hours spent in Rockhampton pubs, riotous adventures with two local journalists, a party for a bevy of chorus beauties aboard the *Sirocco* ("a merry day—with young maidens everywhere from stem to stern"); however the £5 ring fracas of Bundaberg is moved northward to become a feature of carnival week in Rockhampton.

Between Rockhampton and Townsville, a run of some five hundred miles, the *Sirocco* and its exhausted crew relaxed after four weeks of festive living. They drifted among the beautiful islands of the Great Barrier Reef, lay naked on the deck in the warm sun, dined on coconuts and fish, and swam in clear blue water, always maintaining a wary lookout for sharks. On one of these islands they met the Wilson family whose eldest daughter was a stunning primitive beauty. Lucy, age twenty, had never seen the mainland and knew nothing of civilization, but proved an apt and willing pupil. Both Rex and Errol went to work as teachers, and by the time they were ready to leave Lucy was determined she would follow Flynn (the winner) wherever he went. She even swam after the *Sirocco* and clambered aboard.

This prompted a tempestuous scene as the crew tried to convince young Lucy to return home. In the midst of this confrontation Errol vowed he had wrestled manfully with his conscience concerning this innocent child of nature. Rex greeted this lofty assertion with scorn, claiming Flynn failed to score only because of poor technique and added that they might as well let "the little slut" stay. Angered, Errol lashed out with his swift right and knocked Rex to the deck; however, Charlie Burt stepped in and reminded them that brawling was hardly the way out of their dilemma. Eventually they cornered Lucy Wilson, threw a blanket over her head to subdue flailing arms, and left her sobbing on the beach, "trussed up like a fowl". As the four young men rowed silently back to the *Sirocco* in the dinghy, Errol called a soft "goodbye" to his distraught island beauty.

Perhaps as a reaction to this high drama, Flynn was soon back in his bunk suffering from another recurrence of malaria. His condition became so serious that the ship put into the little town of Bowen in search of medical aid. Unable to secure a doctor, they sailed on to Townsville where the skipper spent three days in the local hospital. To earn money the rest of the crew took tourists out to nearby Magnetic Island—until the harbor master warned them they must desist or get a license.

*En route* to Cairns, the next port, the voyagers stopped at Hinchinbrook Island where Charlie Burt visited a friend named Forsythe who (with Burt) had once been co-owner of the *Sirocco*. Forsythe, a legendary character whose exploits were known throughout all of New Guinea, proved to be a very entertaining host. An Eton and Oxford man who had spent some months in prison, he told his enthralled guests about years in Dutch New Guinea where he dabbled in prospecting, illicit trade in bird of paradise feathers, and other nefarious pursuits.

In Cairns, the last major outpost on the Australian coast, high adventure continued at a dizzy pace. There was a fan-tan game which ended in a head-smashing brawl between sugarcane-cutters and Chinese patrons. Rex almost tangled with a shark while swimming to shore from the boat. ("Dook" often rowed the dinghy to the nearby wharf, tied it up, and then forgot about his buddies stranded aboard the yacht.) At the suggestion of a well-to-do Chinese merchant they became opium smugglers; and, when the merchant failed to pay for services rendered, the foursome stole his dinghy. This not only settled accounts to their satisfaction (if not his) but also replaced their small boat which was becoming a leaky nuisance.

However, one of the most intriguing aspects of the visit to Cairns is a tour Rex and Errol made to Mareeba. Flynn writes that the town was "several hundred miles from the coast" and describes in his inimitable technicolor prose the hectic rail journey which ensued. They made the twenty-six hour trip in a quaint, antiquated relic with hard seats and no comforts whatsoever. Upon arrival at Mareeba Flynn planned to borrow horses and ride to a friend's tobacco farm some two hours away; but, exhausted by the long trip, Rex and he went to a hotel to clean up, fell asleep, and did not awake until nearly twenty-four hours later, just in time to catch the train back to the coast.

The return journey was, if anything, worse than the trip inland. The train was packed with sweaty Italians, scores of screaming children, and hordes of hardy outback residents heading for a race meeting to be held in Cairns. Sitting on their suitcases in crowded, cramped conditions, the two travelers became so uncomfortable that they deserted the so-called passenger carriage for a small but well-ventilated cattle car. This ordeal lasted not twenty-six, but *thirty-six* hours.

As any resident of eastern Australia will readily agree, riding the rails of Queensland can be a unique experience even today. Seats often are hard, facilities primitive, and trains slow . . . but not *that* slow! Mareeba, situated on the beautiful tableland above Cairns, is only forty miles from the coast. Even the trains of northern Queensland maintain average speeds in excess of 1.1 to 1.25 miles per hour. As we shall see, this is by no means the last example of Flynn's very inadequate grasp of his surroundings. For a man who traveled great distances on land and sea he appears to have been utterly oblivious to the realities of geography; or, perhaps he thought that, while writing for the insular northern hemisphere reader, he could take considerable liberty with the map of Australia and New Guinea . . . and he does. There is yet another possibility: Errol Flynn simply believed that a good, entertaining story could take precedence over truth.

Disregarding the overlay of exaggerated detail, this story of the trip to Mareeba is not without importance. In 1930 that community was becoming a prime tobacco growing center; and, if Flynn actually did go there as he claims, this visit may well have stirred his imagination. For, a year later he would begin development of one of Papua's earliest tobacco plantations in the hills in back of Port Moresby.

The final stop on the Australian mainland was at Cooktown in mid-August. A roaring mining town with a population of 25,000 in the 1870s, it has been declining steadily throughout the twentieth century and, even when Errol and his friends called there four decades ago, presented a rather dreary sight. Great stone buildings stood forlorn and deserted; herds of goats roamed through the streets. One individual served as harbor master, mayor, and police sergeant. This triple-threat man proved to be an amiable sort and quickly joined the *Sirocco*'s crew in one of Cooktown's many pubs. Errol noted that community must have been the most "bepubbed" town in all of Australia in 1930: fifty-nine watering holes for only three hundred souls.

Bert Weston, the man who built the airfield at Lae, substantiates some of Flynn's observations concerning Cooktown. As a passenger on a pioneer flight which landed there in the late thirties he was struck by the fact that the customs official who met the plane doubled as postmaster; and, according to rumor, he was also station master when a little train limped in once a week from Laura, some seventy miles from the coast.

At Cooktown the *Sirocco* stocked up on provisions for the long hop to New Guinea. These supplies included a goat, some stolen chickens, and other such goodies. The yacht stopped briefly at Lizard Island where the crew found a family near starvation. After ministering to their needs the four adventurers headed out into the Coral Sea.

While this bit of good Samaritanism may be founded on fact, it sounds suspiciously like the tale of Mary Beatrice Watson (1859-81) whose exploits are commemorated by a Cooktown monument. In 1880 she went with her husband, a bêche-de-mer fisherman, to live on Lizard Island. In September of 1881, while Watson was away, their home was attacked by a band of aborigines. One Chinese servant was killed and another injured. Mary bundled her infant son and the wounded servant into a portion of an iron tank and escaped to an outlying reef. When drinking water gave out she rowed the group to other islands, but eventually all members of the harassed little party died of thirst. When found some weeks later their remains were taken to Cooktown where a huge funeral was held and a monument erected to commemorate the tragedy. Errol perhaps pondered this poignant marker during his days there and learned of Lizard Island and the Watsons from local residents:

Once into the open sea and no longer sheltered by the Great Barrier Reef, the *Sirocco* faced sailing conditions reminiscent of those experienced between Sydney and Brisbane; however, after several hectic days the southern coast of New Guinea was sighted. With the assistance of natives they got their bearings and charted a coastal route toward Port Moresby which lay some distance to the northwest.

On the way Flynn decided to stop at a small trading station located in the village of Tavai. At the water's edge eager to greet them was the owner, an eccentric white man named Goodyear. Brown as a native and flashing a dramatic mane of flowing white hair, he insisted they be his guests in a thatched dwelling about half a mile away. Flynn tells us it was a comfortable home, if crude, filled with rickety furniture and assorted animals. ("It quite took me back to Ireland for a moment.") These adventures were Goodyear's first visitors in three months and words flowed in a torrent from his lips.

When it came time to eat, the host placed a long revolver on the table at his right hand, invoked the benevolent blessing of the Almighty upon what they were about to receive, dropped his false teeth into a glass of water with a resounding splash, and with gusto went to work on the first course. It was an excellent fish soup served up by two attractive native girls naked to the waist. All the time Goodyear was babbling on, occasionally warding off a pet parrot as it swooped low over the table. Suddenly he reached for the revolver, took quick aim, and shot past Flynn's head. Errol heard a cry of pain and turned just in time to see a dark form disappearing into the jungle.

"Dirty black thief! I got him!" laughed Goodyear. While his horrified guests exchanged furtive glances their host explained it didn't really hurt much, just an air pistol; but this was the only way he could protect his property.

> If I didn't have this they'd steal every damn thing I've got in my store. I always aim for the arse—if I score a bull's eye, I win a cigar. Ha, ha. Then all they've got to do is go back to their village and dig the slug out.

But dinner was not yet over and the best was still to come. The cook, a husky black savage, appeared and placed a huge cauldron in the center of the table. With keen relish Goodyear lifted the lid to reveal an amazing sight. There surrounded by potatoes and half floating in a dark liquid was the corpse of a wallaby, a small species of kangaroo. Errol tells us the animal was complete with fur, eyes, and teeth and stared moodily at the astonished guests "with a look of deep reproach". Flynn says he was so overcome that he had to get up and leave the table. While standing outside trying to recover he heard Goodyear's booming voice, "Shot him myself two days ago. Hope he hasn't gone bad yet. D'you like a leg?"

Our imaginative reporter doesn't disclose who ate what (if anything); but, according to Allen Innes, the Salamaua hotel and store keeper, Goodyear was so furious when *Beam Ends* appeared that he tried to sue Flynn, but because of international complications finally gave up. What specific bit of Errol's lurid prose distressed him the most is not known—plunking false teeth into a glass, winging natives in the ass, or serving up potted wallaby. Even if the tale of this unusual dinner party is remotely true, it is hardly the way to treat a gracious, well-meaning host.

While much of what Errol Flynn writes in *Beam Ends* should be viewed with healthy skepticism (references to Ireland, faulty geography, constant and unending revelry), the last two chapters are clearly out-and-out fiction. In the first of these (XVII) he describes a slow, two-week cruise from Tavai towards Port Moresby, a distance of only twenty-five miles. Virtually the same material can be found in the pages of the Sydney *Bulletin* of 1932. During a brief career as a contributor to that well-known weekly Flynn submitted several short articles from New Guinea. It is quite apparent that, when putting his first book together a few years later, he dusted off those old clippings and adapted them to his immediate needs.

The concluding chapter is even more suspect. Only a couple of days out of Moresby near the village of Bukausip (not cited in the very thorough gazeteer of the Southwest Pacific published by the United States Board of Geographic Names in 1956) a cyclone suddenly swooped down on the *Sirocco* anchored about half a mile off shore. In the wild moments which followed the fifty-year-old craft broke free and, despite valiant efforts by her sturdy crew, was dashed to bits on a coral reef. Rex, Charlie, and Errol managed to scramble into the new dinghy appropriated from the Cairns opium magnate. In the confusion, however, poor "Dook"—"kindly, lovable old Dock"—was lost forever in the churning, wild-thrashed foam of the angry ocean. His body was never found.

> The *Sirocco*'s bones and his are scattered over a coral reef in the South Seas, as are the bones of many a fine ship, but never of a finer man.

A very touching tribute indeed, but this spectacular flourish of wind, disaster, and sudden death is completely false. The venerable *Sirocco* may have ended her days on a jagged reef, but this did not happen during the cruise from Sydney to Port Moresby. As for dear departed "Dook", he spent the next few years as a schooner captain in New Guinea waters and was a partner in Errol's tobacco venture, 1931-2. Charlie Burt presumably disappeared into the gold fields, and early in 1931 Rex Long-Innes returned to Sydney with Flynn.

Before the more energetic half of the *Sirocco*'s crew set out for Australia (via commercial steamer) there was still time for one more adventure. On Thursday, 10 December, Errol and Rex put to sea with a popular Port Moresby barmaid. Once more there was engine trouble. Two days later this report from New Guinea appeared in the *Sydney Morning Herald*.

> It is feared that the launch *Sirocco*, which smashed on to the reef at Taurama Point this morning, will become a total wreck. Fortunately its three occupants reached shore safely.
>
> The launch is owned by Messrs. Errol Flynn and Rex Longines [*sic*], and came to Port Moresby three

months ago from Sydney. Last night she proceeded to Taurama Point and left early this morning with Miss Anne Haywood as a passenger. About 10 o'clock the oil pipe broke, putting the engine out of action, and the anchor was dropped off Tavai. Flynn and Longines were working at the engine when the anchor carried away, and it was decided to return to Port Moresby with the aid of sails. A heavy sea was running when the launch rounded Taurama Point, and, unable to make headway, the craft crashed heavily on to the reef.

After many attempts to launch the dinghy, the party swam ashore, landing at Pari village, where the natives made a fire to dry their clothes. None of them is any worse for the experience. The tide has since risen, but the launch remains fast on the reef, and little hope is held out for her salvage.

Once more the *Sirocco*'s obituary proved to be premature. The last item which Errol contributed to the *Bulletin* (5 October, 1932) tells how the boat was repaired following this disaster and "is now destined to be a diving-tender, in the bêche-de-mer industry".

Ironically the morbid twist which Flynn added to *Beam Ends*, coupled with the minor incident of December 1930, rebounded to his disadvantage. New Guinea residents of four decades ago who did not like this handsome, smooth-talking upstart (and there were many) are certain the future movie idol was such a cowardly scoundrel that he once failed to save a close friend from drowning when their boat capsized. Those who tell this tale usually identify the victim as Rex Long-Innes. While obviously untrue, it is of such stuff that legends are made; and Errol Flynn, barely twenty-one years of age, was already becoming an integral part of New Guinea folklore.

# Chapter Four

## Pioneer Tobacco Planter of Papua, 1931-1932

On 7 January, 1931, Errol and Rex left Port Moresby for Sydney on the *Morinda*. They arrived there on the 14th, and two weeks later Mr. and Mrs. R. Campbell Dibbs of Bowral and Temora announced the engagement of their daughter Naomi to Errol Thomson Flynn, only son of Professor and Mrs. T. Thomson Flynn of Hobart, Tasmania. A lovely picture of the bride-to-be, revealing a proud, aristocratic young lady, appeared in Sydney's *Daily Pictorial* on 26 January. A brief commentary noted that Naomi had recently returned from Europe and added that Mrs. R. Campbell Dibbs and her daughters had taken a flat at the "Manar" in the Macleay Street section of King's Cross for a time. This news of romance inaugurated a gay round of festivities which included cocktail parties, afternoons of tennis at Nancy Houston's home at Burradoo, and weekends in Bowral. Errol rode the crest of this gay whirl for three months, returning to Port Moresby on the *Morinda* on 30 April.

One can merely conjecture as to what effect (if any) impending marriage had upon Flynn. More apparent is the influence these weeks in Sydney had upon his immediate future. Australia was agog with talk of fortunes being made in tobacco in northern Queensland, especially at Mareeba which Flynn says he visited briefly in August of 1930. Errol, ever on the lookout for quick, easy money, immediately became interested. Commenting on this tobacco boom, the Melbourne *Argus* reported early in 1931 that investment in the Atherton

Tableland area above Cairns was returning a 200% profit. Why not a tobacco plantation in the islands?

In contrast to coconuts, one did not have to wait years for trees to mature. Natives in the area had been growing the crop in a haphazard manner for centuries, yet annually Papua and mandated New Guinea imported cigarettes, cigars, and processed leaf in huge quantities. Long twists were standard issue for all local labor. Each year between 1926 and 1931 Papua alone imported tobacco worth £25,000 to £30,000. This represented (in value) nearly 10% of all imports.

A few miles from Port Moresby in the first ridge of hills which quickly build up into mountain ranges Errol found the perfect site for his plantation. The property, located near picturesque Rouna Falls on the Laloki River, apparently belonged to Beatrice Grimshaw, an Irish-born journalist and author who had fallen in love with the South Seas a decade or so earlier. Although the *Papuan Courier* of Port Moresby (13 January, 1933) reported Miss Grimshaw had purchased this property from Flynn and Trelawney Adams, there are indications she may have been the actual owner some years earlier.

In the early 1920s this well-known writer lived at Samarai in eastern Papua, but by 1930 she had settled in Port Moresby, a community of only four hundred whites. There she became a major social-intellectual influence and close friend of Sir Hubert Murray, lieutenant-governor of Papua from 1907 until his death in 1940. In *Isles of Adventure* (London, 1930) Miss Grimshaw brags of being the first white woman to venture up the Fly and Sepik rivers, tells of tobacco grown by Sepik head-hunters (fair quality . . . good enough for some white men to use in their cigars), and describes her home in Port Moresby and a four-room cottage she owned near Rouna Falls.

In addition to using land which may have belonged to Beatrice Grimshaw, Flynn had the backing of a number of Port Moresby residents who, like he, thought there was quick money to be made in tobacco. Prominent among this group were Dr. William Eric Giblin, a tropical disease specialist, and his wife, Veronica Maria ("Vera"), a couple destined to have a profound effect upon Errol's life. Dr. Giblin's ancestors were among Australia's earliest settlers, having arrived in Hobart Town in 1820. Like Miss Grimshaw, the doctor and his wife had lived in Samarai in the early 1920s, but later moved to Port Moresby.

From mid-1931 until he left the islands in February 1933, the Giblins became Errol Flynn's *de facto* parents and were among his staunchest defenders. He was often in their home; and, in contrast to many local residents, they thought this handsome, wayward youngster had considerable potential. The Giblins are now dead, but their son Dexter (also a doctor) recalls distinctly the great faith his parents placed in Flynn. The younger Giblin, who lives in the Sydney suburb of Wahroonga, concedes they recognized Errol's faults, but claims they saw redeeming features as well.

> Mind you. Let me say this to you. A lot of people were jealous of him, too. He was a young, attractive person. The natives looked up to him. They like people who are young. Good figure. Dressed well . . . white shorts and all. Always very presentable. The natives certainly admired him.

Dexter adds that his mother refused to hear a word against Errol Leslie Thomson Flynn. She often said, "If this man is directed along the right channels he can go a long way." "Mother was right", he chuckles, "although he got a bit sidetracked." Giblin says this close relationship lasted throughout much of the 1930s, and after he got to Hollywood both the star and his first wife, Lili Damita, often wrote to his parents. Frequently they enclosed publicity photos with messages written on the back. One of these from Flynn bestowed lavish praise upon Vera Giblin: "You've done more for me than anybody on this earth!"

Ken Hunter-Kerr confirms that Mrs. Giblin was one of the individuals who backed Errol's tobacco experiment. Trelawney Adams was also a partner in this venture, but only in a financial sense. Instead of tending rows of plants, the young Cambridge graduate roamed the Papuan coast as skipper of the *Royal Endeavour* and the *Ronald S.*, vessels operated by J. R. Clay & Do. Ltd. On several occasions Flynn joined Adams on excursions up the rivers which dot the region. These included trips to Kaparoko in late November of 1931 and to Kikori in May of 1932. Will Jefferson, owner of the Ogamobu rubber plantation, was his Kikori host, a role which Jefferson apparently enjoyed less and less as Flynn's visit lengthened into several weeks. A year later Jefferson entertained John Vandercook whose *Dark Islands* (London, 1938) describes delightful days spent at Ogamobu.

Errol's five-acre Laloki venture even had the blessing of local officialdom—a state of affairs unique in such a rough-and-tumble career. In his annual report (1931-2) Sir Hubert Murray quoted his acting director of agriculture on tobacco growing. A. P. Lyons said it was not new to the territory. There had been failures in Australia, too, but now crops were doing extremely well in Queensland.

> There is no reason that I know of why it should not be made so in Papua, for undoubtedly we have the land, climate, and other natural advantages, besides cheap labour, and we can find a good market in the United Kingdom.

During late 1931 and early 1932 Errol and his boys worked hard over the crop, although *My Wicked, Wicked Ways* indicates Flynn may have spent more time at dalliance with the lovely "Tuperselai" whom he says he purchased for two pigs, a "fuse" of English shillings, and some seashell money. Perhaps. Anyway, tobacco plants warrant about one page of text; "Tuperselai" gets three and one-half. This maiden, "almost scentless, a bit like hibiscus", apparently came from or was inspired by the coastal village of Tupuselei, a few miles south of Port Moresby and not far from Laloki.

On 5 April, 1932, Jack Hides, a flamboyant patrol officer, noted in his diary that he arrived at Flynn's plantation at 1 p.m.

> At the kind invitation of Mr. Flynn, the patrol camped for the night at the tobacco plantation. During the afternoon I visited the curing plant and saw over a ton of tobacco classed for export. I believe Mr. Flynn is exporting a ton of cured tobacco during the next week.

In *The Outside Man: Jack Hides of Papua* (Melbourne, 1969), James Sinclair comments that the two men possessed marked similarities. Flynn was somewhat larger, but both were tall, slim, good-looking, had easy, natural charm, and sported thin moustaches. They met from time to time in Port Moresby pubs, and one drinking session ended in a good-natured fight which Flynn won easily enough.

In the mid-1930s Hides would become something of a folk hero as a result of exploration, writing, and lecture tours in Australia; however, resulting publicity received a cool reception from the Papuan administration. In July of 1936 he resigned from government service and began searching for gold, backed by a Sydney syndicate. Two years later "Jack-a-Hide", as his native admirers called him, died suddenly of pneumonia.

Despite the benign attitude of the local authorities and Jack Hides report of substantial output, Flynn's tobacco venture was not a success. What went wrong is not entirely clear. In his annual report for the year ending 30 June, 1932, Sir Hubert Murray said 2,085 pounds of raw tobacco had been exported from Papua. Presumably this was the tobacco Hides saw at Laloki in April of that year. In 1933 Sir Hubert said the result of the previous year's sale on the London market had not been satisfactory. "It is now known that the curing of the leaf was faulty, hence the unfavourable result."

Yet, to some extent Errol was the victim of a political hassle. Australia seemed to be the natural market for his crop, but that outlet was closed to him. At about the time he was processing his leaf, officials in Canberra reduced the import duty from 5/2 to 3/- per pound. Federal parliamentarians wrangled over this issue for seven hours and managed to fill fifty-four pages in the *Debates*, but the government proposal to reduce the tariff finally won out, much to the disgust of hundreds of Australian growers. Ostensibly this move might have helped Flynn. A mere 2,085 pounds of Papuan tobacco was not going to cause much of a flutter on the market.

It appears, however, that Canberra was not about to encourage any colonial crop which might hurt home production in the future . . . or, perhaps Errol should have considered more closely the words of A. P. Lyons (local director of agriculture) who had said Papuan tobacco would find a ready market in the United Kingdom. Whatever the reasons, Papua's incipient tobacco magnate could not sell any part of his crop in Australia, and he was (quite naturally) furious. On 20 July he vented his displeasure in a hard-hitting letter published in the *Bulletin*, Australia's best-known weekly.

> *Dear Bulletin.*—Papua is one of the natural homes of the tobacco plant, and, as Papua is part of the Commonwealth and is in receipt of a yearly subsidy of $40,000 from the Federal Government, the obvious market for its tobacco is Australia. But the market is closed by a prohibitive tariff. Within the past eight months the Papuan Government twice made representations to Canberra on behalf of a pioneering tobacco-growing concern, asking for a preference over foreign countries. It was pointed out that Papua is part of the Commonwealth, supported by the Australian taxpayer, and that a reasonable preference would perhaps mean the beginning of a large and profitable industry; also that Papua, with the bottom fallen out of

two staple commodities (copra and rubber), is urgently in need of a new industry. The reply in both cases was identical—the matter was being given consideration. They have apparently been considering it ever since, for the Papual Government has heard no more of the matter. Meanwhile the pioneering concern has produced a splendid crop just behind Port Moresby, which is being sent to the English market, as the growers can no longer afford to await the decision of the procrastinating authorities in Canberra. It would be a near-sighted policy should the fact that the tobacco was grown by black labour prevent those responsible from assisting Papua in every way possible, when that country is being expensively supported by the Australian taxpayer. And particularly when, as in this case, the assistance would not harmfully affect Australia, which is still and must be for years a large importer of leaf.

Yours, ERROL FLYNN (Papua)

Flynn's points are well phrased indeed, especially his sly reference to an anti-black mentality in Canberra; but, according to residents of the Papua-New Guinea area in the 1920s and 1930s, his experience was all too typical. Australian officialdom rarely displayed much interest in the potential of the region. Ironically, few islanders ever read this outburst. The *Bulletin* didn't circulate widely there . . . not because of editorial policy or general content, but because it was printed on smooth, glossy paper. Allen Innes recalls that plantation owners, recruiters, and traders were always hard-pressed to supply cigarette "paper" for their boys.

Natives wouldn't have anything to do with the *Bulletin*. They wouldn't smoke it. Didn't like the taste of it. They preferred newsprint. The *Sydney Morning Herald* smoked good, Boys liked it.

Flynn's letter of protest was not his sole contribution to the *Bulletin* during these months, although it is the only one bearing his name. Using the *nom de plume* of "Laloki" he placed at least seven items on the "Aboriginalities" page, a regular feature of that weekly. In *My Wicked, Wicked Ways* Errol tells us he was the *Bulletin's* Papuan correspondent and that the editors sent him £20 for his work. Wrong on one count, perhaps two. In those days, regardless of where they lived, writers had to go to the *Bulletin's* Sydney offices in person to collect payment for their published efforts. And £20 sounds unusually generous.

Errol also entertains us with a wonderful tale of how he decided to promote his tobacco empire by taking a group of natives to Sydney. Somehow this troupe was supposed to help him make a stock "float" among interested Sydney investors. He tells us of his hilarious arrival armed with propositions for the expansion of his plantation and accompanied by eight Papuans decked out in feathers, flowers, and cloth-wrapped penises. As they approached the city Errol decided to dress each one in sailor pants. Once ashore the natives gawked, giggled, and shrieked at all the wonders of white man's "big smoke". Flynn even quotes the headlines of the *Bulletin's* story on this spectacular sight:

## MR. FLYNN RETURNS FROM NEW GUINEA WITH COMPANY OF PAPUANS

### He is Here to Make Stock Flotation in Tobacco

Neither these headlines nor any story about Flynn's tobacco empire appear to have been printed in Sydney.

Our would-be magnate describes a fantastic visit to Anthony Hordern's department store with Anitok, one of the natives. Anitok and this same tale appear in *Showdown*. It seems Anitok tried to buy cloth, but when his money disappeared on an overhead wire to make change he thought he was being robbed and pandemonium erupted throughout the emporium. In *My Wicked, Wicked Ways* Flynn takes full credit for restoring order; in *Showdown* Anitok was on his own and chased the metal container as far as he could. Failing to catch it, he simply walked away, convinced that the white man had cheated him once more. In his novel Flynn also describes Anitok's equally unfortunate visit to a Sydney whorehouse. Out of these experiences come (not unexpectedly) Anitok's hatred of the white man and his ways, a major theme in the story line developed in *Showdown*.

After a few more days of movies and other wonders of civilization Errol says he rounded up his colorful companions and shipped them back to Papua. He then got down to the hard task of creating interest in his tobacco scheme, but without much success. Hot on the heels of this defeat Flynn proceeds to describe events which actually occurred while he was *en route* to England early in 1933. This prompts a natural conclusion that tales of a tobacco float and the trip to Sydney with a band of ex-head-hunters are largely fiction.

It is quite possible that Flynn made some feeble efforts in mid-1932 (or earlier) to interest Sydney investors in a tobacco enterprise of some sort. H. R. Niall says, in fact, that much of the money for the initial venture came from the syndicate formed in the Port Moresby area in 1931. ("This was a failure and everybody concerned lost their investments.") It is equally possible that Errol witnessed the reactions of Papuan natives to the wonders of Sydney during one of his visits there . . . but these events clearly did not take place in 1933 as indicated . . . and perhaps they did not take place at all.

But, to return to Errol Flynn's "Laloki" items in the *Bulletin*. The first was published on 2 December, 1931, and the last (the seventh) appeared on 5 October, 1932. They cover a wide range of subjects and the final contribution tells us what the future holds for the *Sirocco*. Two of these items were incorporated into *Beam Ends*. Errol's first book published in 1937. Reproduced here in chronological sequence they reveal both Flynn's interest in native life and his natural skills as story-teller, observer, and writer.

The result of the pourri-pourri seance in Port Moresby (B. 28/10/31), at which medicine men enjoying great prestige among the surrounding tribes failed to bring a dead dog back to life, should have been a moral victory for his Ex. But the Papuan sorcerer is an astute opportunist. The chief pourri-pourri expert suddenly remembered that the medical officer, invited to satisfy himself that the dog was dead, had touched it with his stethoscope. That, of course, cleared up the mystery of the dog's refusal to come to life. Every reasonable native knew at once that the medical officer had applied a powerful counter pourri-pourri. It is unfortunately true that the magicians were given presents of rice and flour—a not unusual instance of official stupidity. If these natives did not return to their village and exhibit the rice and flour as proof that the Government was much impressed with their prowess, then they're not the pourri-pourri men I take them for. They ought to be able to live on their reputation in ease and luxury for the rest of their lives.

(2 December, 1931, p. 21)

Killing a turtle in New Guinea is a horribly messy business. I once came upon several natives about to dispatch a 600 lb. specimen. The turtle was lying on its back on the beach, helplessly flapping, and my cook-boy, Mai-Iki, squatted nearby, kindling a fire on its stomach. Bellowing loudly I rushed to the rescue, scattered the fire, and, in honest rage, was about to inflict grievous bodily harm on Mai-Iki. Deciding, however, that he knew no better, I sent a boy for my revolver, and, while awaiting him, discoursed to the assembly on the evil of cruelty to animals. To my annoyance Mai-Iki wanted to debate the matter. 'Master,' he said earnestly, 'this fella he so savvy die quick time. S'pose you shoot 'im he no die.' 'No?' I said, you watch, and pumped three rounds from a .32 into its head. To my chagrin the turtle showed no sign of having noticed anything unusual, and did not even interrupt the slow pendulum-like movement of its head from side to side. Rather staggered by such unconcern I fired three more rounds, but with the same result. The thing seemed slightly bored with the proceedings and certainly displayed no resentment. '

Bring akis!' (bring an axe) I shouted desperately. 'Cut off head belong 'im.' That was done and the turtle, I thought, was out of its dreadful agony. But when, to my amazement, the headless body continued to breathe through the severed windpipe, as though losing a head was an everyday occurrence, I threw the towel in. 'All right,' I told Mai-Iki, 'go ahead and kill it anyway you like.' He remade the fire, and when the tissue was no longer like leather cut the flesh around the edge and removed the stomach shell, leaving the inside exposed. It was such an uncanny sight to see the heart pumping and everything else apparently working to schedule that I repaired to the house for a drink. Even when I returned several hours later the turtle wasn't quite dead.

(27 January, 1932, p. 20)

The Kuku-kukus were the cause of many unpleasant alarms to the party of Europeans who for the last year have been prospecting in the headwaters of the Taveri River in Western Papua. The white men never slept, ate, worked or performed their toilet without a revolver close at hand. When contact could be established, safety-razor blades were found to be the best 'trade', but at first six wax matches would buy 20 lb. of native food for carriers. These, however, the Kuku-kukus soon eschewed, due to the fact that they would immediately strike the matches one after another, to the immense delight of their relations, and then have nothing left to show for the food they had sold. When the used matches failed to ignite a second time they regarded it as a callous swindle and demanded the return of the food, this being refused an ugly situation was barely averted. Culturally the Kukuk-kukus are still in the Stone Age. Tools and implements are all made of stone, and the clearing of a few acres of timber is arduous toil. It takes them a week to fell one tree, 2 ft. in diameter, so that when they first saw a steel axe in use, one man completing in a day what would take them a month to perform, they were overcome with astonishment. But later on their surprise could not be compared with that of the Europeans when two mysterious Kukuk-kuku implements were found. A steel axe head, presumably stolen, had been cut through and the two halves thus procured were fastened with lawyer vine to handles formed like the figure 7. The result was two adze-shaped implements, and these, with other tools which were found, made from shovels cut in pieces, greatly intrigued the Europeans, who wondered how these primitive people had contrived to cut steel. It was concluded that the steel had been sawn or rather worn through with incredible patience by means of a length of lawyer vine and sand, a conjecture which, if correct, will make the ant, which has so long served as a model of industry, appear as a futile dodderer beside the Kukuk-kukus.

(13 April, 1932, p. 21)

The medical officer was making a visit of inspection in the village of Hanuabada, near Port Moresby, and was confronted by a deaf and dumb native. That native had been as garrulous and able to hear as well as any other

Papuan a week or so previously, so the m.o. inquired of the village constable, how he became affected, 'Well,' answered the gentleman cautiously, 'I understand it was a punishment for blasphemy. The man would not listen to the talk of Tau, the missionary, and one day, in Tau's presence, he tore a page from the Bible to use as cigarette-paper. So Tau said he would ask God to strike him deaf and dumb. And God did.' The m.o., who realized he was up against a case of pourri-pourri, sent the sufferer to hospital and there gave him the only possible treatment for his trouble, counter pourri-pourri; and was gratified to see an immediate response. In fact, so sedulously did he cast his spells that the man was completely cured in the course of a day. Later the m.o. learned that the pious Tau had once sought the afflicted one's sister in marriage, and met with a refusal. Tau no longer interprets the Gospel in Hanaubada.

(25 May, 1932, p. 26)

The Motuan language is singularly lacking in vituperative possibilities, but it has one good, very good, word for that purpose. Call a Papuan a 'Goiaribari' and you heap upon him the $n$th degree of loathing and contempt. The Goiaribari people are by far the lowest tribe I have ever come across. In addition to being filthy in all their habits, and eaters of snakes, snails, and crocodiles, their treatment of their womenfolk relegates them to a cultural status little above that of the beast. A Goiaribari will prostitute his wife and daughter to anyone for three sticks of trade tobacco, sell her outright to the highest bidder, or hire her out by the week or month. It is necessary that young man of this tribe about to marry should first do some brave deed. This is how he usually qualified: He purchases from her father, who knows exactly what will happen to her, a girl about 12 years old, and then gathers round him six or seven cronies. The party, armed with spears, stone axes and other weapons, journey into the bush for a week or longer. The girl is, for several days, subjected to unmentionable barbarities. Then, at last, the stalwart braves form a circle about her and, at a signal, all rush in to hack and batter her to pulp. She is then cut into small pieces, cooked in sections of bamboo and eaten. Such a case occurred only a month ago and the murderers are still at large.

(15 June, 1932, p. 20)

A Papuan walked into a trade store in Moresby, planked three shillings on the counter and demanded a 'pyblo.' 'A what?' inquired the European storekeeper. 'What's it like?' The customer explained that he was to appear before the magistrate that afternoon to engage in litigation for the return of his wife, who had deserted him for another, and he wanted to weight the scales of justice as much as possible in his own favour by buying a 'pyblo', which, he felt confident, would serve that end. 'Yes, but what is this pyblo?' insisted the storekeeper. 'Show me what it's like.' 'This one book, Iaubada. 'nother kind book—too strong! Before time I see one Taubada go along courthouse. He got case. First time he go inside courthouse he stand up, he take this one pyblo in his hand, he smell 'im—all right, he win this one case. Ah, 'nother kind book, this one.' The explanation sufficed, and the storekeeper sold him a Bible, an old one, whose efficacy was claimed to be enhanced by age.

(17 August, 1932, p. 20)

One of the oldest yachts in the world, the *Sirocco*, is lying at anchor near Port Moresby in Papua. She was built by Ford in 1881 at his shipyards on Sydney's Circular

Quay for E. W. Knox, of C.S.R. fame. Old-timers remember when, with her blackbearded owner at the tiller and generally one small boy as crew, she developed speed that was the pride of the waterside. She sailed for 34 years before her original sail plan was altered. Her then owner cut several feet from the topmast, shortened her booms and discarded four tons of lead ballast. She sailed as well as previously, and continued a successful racing career for 11 years. When nearly 50 years old she was bought by a New Guinea planter, who sailed her to Papua, taking five months for the journey from Sydney. Her subsequent history included a collision with a coral reef, but she was repaired, and is now destined to be a diving-tender, in the bêche-de-mer industry.

(5 October, 1932, p. 21)

Well, hardly Pulitzer Prize material, but certainly readable stuff. And one should keep in mind that breaking into the page of the *Bulletin* of those days was no minor feat. Every would-be writer viewed that publication as the Olympian heights of Australian journalism. Some even refused to cash their initial check, treasuring it as a prestigious memento. Flynn was undoubtedly less sentimental.

If nothing else, these items from Papua prove that Errol Flynn *could* write and indicate that his three books—although he had considerable assistance with the final one—were essentially his own work. Despite rather casual formal education and a well-developed disdain for classroom training, he clearly learned something about composition at Hutchins, Friends', Hobart High, Shore, etc., etc., etc. Pat Edlershaw, for one, taught much better than he realized.

Late in July of 1932, having shipped his tobacco to England, Errol boarded the *Macdhui* for Sydney, arriving there early on the morning of 5 August. This trip southward may have been prompted by some vague notion to begin a stage career. Dr.

Dexter Giblin recalls that Flynn in those days had "a lovely English voice". Both of his parents often urged their protégé to take full advantage of his natural endowments—good voice, fine physique, commanding presence, and winning charm.

Errol obviously did not know what lay ahead; but, before he again saw Port Moresby some five months later, his rise to fame and fortune would be under way. And do not take the hackneyed phrase "fame and fortune" lightly. His experiences during this Sydney sojourn provide the first rung on the ladder to both—although, as we shall see shortly, monetary gain (even ill-gotten) was perhaps more important to his unfolding career than any fame engendered by a shaky, amateurish film debut. At long last Mrs. Flynn's little boy was, as she wished, finding his slot in the world and getting into something".

# Chapter Five

## Fletcher Christian, Jewels, and . . . Goodbye Australia!

Precisely how Errol spent his first few weeks in the big metropolis is not known, but he soon resumed contacts with his fiancée, friends, and relatives—Naomi, Ken Hunter-Kerr, his grandmothers, and other individuals he knew. *My Wicked, Wicked Ways* is of little help at this point since he resurrects the mythical "Joel Swartz" who presumably cabled (while Flynn was still on his tobacco plantation in Papua) and asked him to come to Tahiti at once to play the role of Fletcher Christian in a movie based on the *Bounty* saga. The closest Errol ever got to beautiful Matavai Bay in 1932 was Bondi Junction in Sydney's eastern suburbs. Strangely, although this episode marks a major turning point in Flynn's career, he garbles the account horribly, almost beyond recognition.

On 27 August, 1932, Charles Chauvel, one of Australia's most talented movie makers with several productions to his credit, returned from a prolonged visit to Pitcairn Island and Tahiti where he, his wife Elsa, and their camera man, Tasman Higgins, shot many reels of film. According to a book which Chauvel published in 1933 bearing the same title as his movie, *In the Wake of the Bounty*, he had been intrigued by the potential of this tale for several years. He first became interested while visiting a descendant of Captain Bligh who owned a Queensland cattle property. There he read Bligh's log of the *Providence* describing a Pacific cruise made from 1791 to 1793, a few years after the *Bounty* affair. During a Hollywood tour in 1930 "the full possibilities of the subject struck me". Mrs. Chauvel says something else also "struck" her husband in America. They went to California with high hopes of selling several short productions; but, unfortunately, their arrival coincided with the advent of sound. Silent films from Down Under were hardly in great demand.

Undaunted, the Chauvels returned to Australia. Charles studied materials relating to the *Bounty* held in Sydney's Mitchell Library and within a year thought he had a workable script. What he had in mind was a documentary describing present-day Pitcairn Island enhanced by a collection of historical scenes designed to explain the background of the famous mutiny.

And how does Errol Flynn enter the story? Years later, at the time of the actor's death, Chauvel said he saw a picture of a young man whose yacht had been wrecked on the Queensland coast. He looked like a perfect Fletcher Christian, and eventually his staff was able to locate Errol. While the *Sirocco* certainly did go aground, that mishap occurred near Port Moresby late in 1930, and it is most unlikely that any photographs of the incident were published. It is true pictures of Flynn and his pals appeared in Sydney's *Daily Pictorial* (17 February, 1930), when the *Sirocco* got into difficulty outside of the Heads; but it is equally unlikely Chauvel would treasure a newspaper clipping for over two years on the mere chance that he *might* make a movie and *perhaps* require the services the services of a completely unknown individual.

It appears instead that Flynn's decision to spend a Sunday on the sands near Bondi was the first step to stardom. John Warwick, now a professional actor of long standing but then casting director for Cinesound Studios, saw Flynn's stalwart form and thought, "My God! There's Fletcher Christian!" Chauvel's Expeditionary Film Company was utilizing Cinesound's facilities, so Warwick was well aware of the search for a leading man. A few days later Warwick telephoned Ken Hunter-Kerr, one of Errol's beach companions, and asked the name and address of that handsome youth who had been with him that day. A meeting with the Chauvels was arranged at the famous Long Bar of the Hotel Australia, and the job was his.

Errol's co-workers included Mayne Lynton as Captain Bligh, Victor Gourier playing the part of a blind fiddler, Patricia Penman as Isabella (for romantic interest), and—strangely—John Warwick in the role of Edward Young, Flynn's distant relative who joined Christian on Pitcairn Island. In his autobiography Errol says he worked on the film for about three weeks "without the least idea of what I was doing except that I was supposed to be an actor".

As filming progressed during September and October, some unexpected difficulties arose. On 26 September Charles Chauvel told a *Sydney Morning Herald* reporter that Australian censors (they appear to have been even more ridiculous forty years ago) had denied entry to the Pitcairn-Tahiti footage *in toto*. Three weeks later he conceded he would have to edit the scenes in question and resubmit them for approval. It is no surprise to learn that Polynesian dance sequences were the source of his troubles. At the same time Chauvel announced that indoor work was nearly complete and the cast would soon move to a ship in the harbour.

Elsa Chauvel, who starred in her husband's productions in the 1920s and subsequently served as his "right hand man" in a score of capacities, thought Flynn "a fantastic romancer". Give him a role, make-up, and a costume and shortly he would convince himself he actually was related to the individual he was portraying. In the case of Fletcher Christina, as we've seen, this conviction had some basis in fact. Mrs. Chauvel says Errol, "a kind of male butterfly", simply "breezed into our lives, caused trouble with the girls in the studio, and left".

The Chauvels did not see him again until 1955 when they were in London editing one of their most successful productions, *Jedda*. They contacted an old friend, Anna Neagle, who was making a movie with Flynn. (This film was *Lilacs in Spring*, released in America as *Let's Make Up*.) She, in turn, told the star that the Chauvels were in London, and, he and his wife, Patrice Wymore, staged a glittering dinner party in their honor at the Savoy.

Years later Mrs. Chauvel recalled Errol's jaunty introduction of her husband, Charles, who died in 1959 shortly after Flynn.

"I want to tell you folks something—This little fella from Down Under once had the nerve to pay me £10 a week!" Amid the laughter of the guests came Chauvel's rejoiner: "And I can tell you something—in those days you were getting £2 more than the producer!"

By early November of 1932 Errol Flynn's first professional experience before the camera had ended, and even his island pals knew about his new career. On 4 November Port Moresby's *Papuan Courier* reprinted this rather cruel paragraph from Kitten's "Catty Communications", first published in *Smith's Weekly* (22 October, 1932).

> Errol Flynn, the tall good-looking lad who is engaged to Naomi Dibbs, has been selected by Charles Chauvel to play an important role in his talkie. 'The Mutiny on the Bounty', and I hear he photographs and records quite wonderfully. What a pity Naomi couldn't get a 'break', too, as I've heard she thinks she is another Garbo. Some of her creations certainly out-Hollywood Hollywood.

The Port Moresby editor headlined this item "Papuan Tobacco Planter Becomes a Talkie Artist". Undoubtedly some readers thought these words uniquely appropriate.

The Fletcher Christian opus was not a rousing success, but by the time *In the Wake of the County* was being screened before Australian audiences Flynn was thousands of miles away *en route* to England. He tells us in his autobiography that he happened to be in Sydney during the premiere and appeared each night at the theater in a bizarre, out-dated British uniform and a blonde wig, earning £3 per show. Not true.

During the closing months of 1932 and January and February of 1933 Chauvel flooded the press with tales of Pitcairn and Tahiti and continued to do battle with the censors. Finally, on 15 March 1933, the movie opened at Sydney's Prince Edward Theatre. This large ad in the *Sydney Morning Herald* hailed the extravaganza.

## ACTUALLY PHOTOGRAPHED ON PITCAIRN ISLAND AND TAHITI

Never did a picture prove more definitely that truth is stranger than fiction. All the thrill of mutiny on the high seas, when Lieutenant Christian sets Commander Bligh of the *Bounty* adrift in a rowing boat! The excitement of the unknown when the little band discover the island of Pitcairn! The charms of the exotic when the sirens of the islands woo these sea-faring adventurers with the beauty of their native dances will set your pulses tingling, too. And then the dreadful aftermath of all their revelry! It will hold you spellbound.

The same program included the Prince Edward Corps de Ballet, orchestra and organ numbers, short subjects, and *Society's Shame*, a comedy film featuring the Nawab of Pataudi (a celebrated cricket star), Cyril Ritchard, and Madge Elliott.

The *Sydney Mail*, a weekend magazine published by the *Sydney Morning Herald*, thought the production "one of the best of Australian talkies"; but, since it was also one of the first made on that continent, this comment means little. The *Mail's* reviewer found the acting of Lynton and Flynn "completely adequate . . . an exceptionally interesting and novel picture judged by any standards". Sydney's *Daily Telegraph* thought it an "ideal" film and commented that the role of Christian was "particularly well acted".

*Smith's Weekly* went into raptures over the Tahitian scenes and showered unrestrained compliments upon the "convincing and natural" acting of Flynn and Lynton. It was a splendid "Australian achievement". The historical sequences were perhaps a bit too brief, bust "excellently done". The *Bulletin*, presumably Flynn's friend, found the effort "disappointing". As a result of bungling censorship the island natives were "not merely clothed, they were overdressed". Only when the camera got to Pitcairn Island did the movie actually come to life, and, as a travelogue the film was certainly up to world standards. This reviewer made no comment upon the acting ability of that magazine's Papuan contributor.

Early in June *In the Wake of the Bounty* opened at Hoyts' Theatre De Luxe in Melbourne on a double bill with a British comedy, "Gene Gerrard in *Let Me Explain, Dear!* The *Argus* called it a "competent film . . . a scenic adventure" in which episodes obviously shot in the confines of the studio contrasted starkly with outdoor footage. Nevertheless, the *Argus* agreed Chauvel's work showed what could be done in that part of the world. The *Age* remarked in passing that the movie featured excellent photography. It closed after one week.

During the remaining months of 1933 the movie played spasmodically in other Australian cities, reaching Hobart in January of 1934. The fact that a hometown boy starred received no publicity in the local press. It was at the Avalon Theatre for six days, playing with an American film—Jean Hersholt, Wayne Gibson, and Stuart Erwin in *The Crime of the Century*. At the rival Strand, Errol's high school passion pit, Joan Blondell and Chester Morris could be seen in *Blondie Johnson*.

Since *In the Wake of the Bounty* moved about the Down Under theatrical circuit at such a leisurely pace and rarely played more than a week or two in any city we can conclude that Flynn, Lynton, and Chauvel were not breaking box office records. Also, it is well-known that Australians of the depression years stayed away from their much-loved cinema palaces by the hundreds whenever a Pommy comedy was playing, hence the Melbourne double bill is not impressive.

The film was never screened before American audiences in its original form. In 1935, when Metro-Goldwyn-Mayer decided to make *Mutiny on the Bounty*, it secured U.S. rights and subsequently released two promotional shorts—*Primitive Pitcairn* and *Pitcairn Today*—which used some of the documentary footage. The camera work of Tasman Higgins won high praise in America. *Variety*, while contemptuous of the acting and a disjointed, jumbled script, thought his obvious skill the highlight of the film.

By mid-November of 1932 Errol Flynn was living in a small rented flat in King's Cross and catching up on the kind of social life Laloki and Port Moresby could not possibly provide. John Warwick tried to interest Ken Hall, boss of Cinesound, in using the young actor in *The Squatter's Daughter*, a film he was putting together, but Hall said no. Then, the chance decision of a local society leader to give a party set the stage for young Flynn's second great adventure in Sydney. This woman—married, very wealthy, and connected with one of that city's commercial dynasties—called Warwick and asked him to round up a few theatrical types to add zest to a mid-week gathering at her home. Warwick was glad to oblige, and among those who enjoyed this lavish hospitality was Fletcher Christian, alias Errol Leslie Thomson Flynn, late of Papua, New Guinea, Tasmania, and so on.

A few days later, on a Saturday morning, the telephone rang in Warwick's flat. It was Naomi Dibbs calling from Bowral. Would Errol be at home over the weekend? Warwick hustled around to Flynn's quarters nearby. (He did not have a phone.) After some delay Errol, disheveled and somewhat irked, answered Warwick's knock. They chatted for a moment; then, Warwick, sizing up the situation and being a good sport, returned to his apartment and told Naomi that her fiancé didn't seem to be at home. He was sure Flynn was not far away, perhaps out on an errand or possibly sailing for the day. Naomi thanked him and replied that, since she couldn't be sure, she would probably not come to Sydney until Monday or Tuesday.

The following week Warwick encountered Errol in "the Cross", and he was bubbling over with sensational news.

"You know who was with me when you dropped by on Saturday, don't you, John?"

"Why, no . . . I really have no way of knowing at all."

"It was our hostess of last Wednesday . . . and something awful happened during the weekend while we were together. Someone entered my flat and took her jewels! And, it's a goddamned mess! She can't go to the police. She told her husband she was going to visit her sister in the country for a few days. So, she's got to replace the loss herself before he finds out about it."

Four decades later it is impossible to know just what Warwick thought of this story as it unfolded. After all, he had only met Errol Flynn a few weeks before. But . . . fade out King's Cross, Sydney, and Australia. Let us transfer our locale to England in the year 1935. Flynn has come, conquered, and gone on to Hollywood, thanks to some incredible luck and the foresight of Warner Brothers. John Warwick, in an effort to advance his own acting career, has moved to London. There he joined a repertory company which had in its ranks a youthful Pommy mouthing the most atrocious Down Under slang one can imagine. Asked who taught him such trash, the actor, named Pete Rosser, replied, "That great Australian film star, Errol Flynn!" Unable to suppress his amazement, Warwick burst out laughing.

"Great Australian film star! Good heavens, I helped him get the only screen role he ever had in Sydney and also played in the production with him. Charles Chauvel's *In the Wake of the Bounty*. You might even say I actually discovered him."

"Yes, I know," replied Rosser, "he talked about that movie a lot. Say, there are some things I would like to ask you about Errol. He came here with a tremendous build-up.

The management called the entire company together, told us this Aussie screen star would join us, and then proceeded to trot out you-know-who. He looked fine, sounded superb, had great style . . . but, frankly, he simply didn't know the first thing about acting. He didn't even know his way around the stage! To top everything, on opening night as we were taking our bows I was standing next to him. Errol turns to me and asks, 'How did I do?' I replied, 'Good. Very good, indeed.' And you know what he does? He smiles that smug, self-satisfied smile of his, gives a debonair tilt to his head, and says, 'What a relief! Pete, this is the *first* time I have ever been on the stage in my entire life!'"

As Warwick and Rosser chatted and compared notes, more details of Errol Flynn in England (and in Australia as well) quickly came to the surface. Rosser reported that their mutual acquaintance lived in high style. He drove an MG, had the best of clothes, and traveled widely. "Of course," the young actor added, "all this was impossible on his salary . . .but he had all those diamonds in his belt!"

All those diamonds! Errol tells a slightly different version of this story in *My Wicked, Wicked Ways*, and one Sydney friend of the early 1930s says the jewels actually were not diamonds, but pearls. But, like dismissal from Dalgety's for plundering the stamp account and other embarrassing twists in his career, the basic elements are all there. In his autobiography he recalls delightfully sensuous hours spent with "Madge Parks", a married woman of the world, who picked him up near Usher's Hotel in Sydney shortly after his job with Chauvel ended. She was auburn-haired, rich, sophisticated. They danced, dined, flirted, swam at the beach, and logged in considerable mattress time.

Then, early one morning as Madge lay sleeping (contently we trust), our vigorous but shaken hero staggered to the bathroom and suddenly realized that his constitution was beginning to crack under the sexual strain. At that moment he turned to look at his voluptuous beauty, but saw instead the dressing table where she had flung her jewels. "Big ones, small ones", he writes, "and there were a couple of rings." A horrible thought crossed his clouded mind. There she lay and there lay the jewels, both lovely and desirable and waiting for him. Flynn concluded he "must" do the dastardly deed and take full advantage of this unusual opportunity which was, after all, merely a short term loan. He would pay Madge back as soon as he could. Overcoming any momentary hesitation and whatever qualms tried to rise, he scooped up the loot, jerked on his pants, stole swiftly down the fire escape, and was away.

Errol tells us he hid the jewels in the handle of a shaving brush and kept telling himself it was a lousy thing to do, stealing from a woman who had befriended him. Sometime in the future, somehow, he would make good her loss. Flynn claims that later, when he became a star, he hired an agency to locate Madge, but never succeeded in doing so. Police were soon on his trail and searched his stateroom as he was leaving Sydney on a north-bound steamer. They found nothing. Then from Brisbane he went whirling off—according to *My Wicked, Wicked Ways*—into a series of bizarre jobs in the Queensland outback.

He joined an unsuccessful well-digging crew at Diamond Downs for two months, then "dagged the hogget" on a huge sheep station until caught in the sack with one of the owner's young daughters who was home from school. Errol describes "dagging the hogget" as the process of cleaning up the tail section preparatory to shearing, but adds a flourish about castrating male animals by biting off their testicles. He had good firm jaws and was "new man" on the scene so *that* was his job; however, experienced sheep men say Flynn was confused "lambing" with dagging" . . . two quite different operations. This rudimentary means of de-sexing is practiced, but on animals a few weeks to three months old. "Lambing" includes cutting off tails, clipping or marking of ears, and castration of males. Actually the testicles are not bitten off, but "sucked out" after the lamb's scrotum has been cut. Similar treatment of a well-developed hogget (a yearling lamb) during shearing time might meet with some objection from the animal concerned.

Of course, good jaws and fine teeth were not necessarily Errol's most promising features. One of the station owner's nubile offspring soon had Flynn off the "dagging" line and on her. Surprised in their rapture by the entrance of Mr. Jack (papa), Errol grabbed his pants, shirt, and shaving brush, murmured a frantic farewell to his love, and was gone!

He eventually made his way to Townsville on the coast . . . broke. Urgent cables to New Guinea went unanswered for forty-eight hours, then money arrived from two friends, Jack Ryan and Vera Giblin. These funds were accompanied by the startling news that he was half owner of a gold lease won in a government lottery. A few days later Flynn arrived in Salamaua feeling a bit like "Diamond Jim Brady". Mrs. Giblin, aged fifty-five, his lottery partner, met him on the pier. They danced a quick jig, sang raucous Papuan songs, and he was off to the gold fiends to seek "their" fortune.

In this sequence Errol Flynn weaves such an intricate web of truth and fiction that it is difficult to know just where to begin the unraveling process. But let's try.

1.  If "Madge Parks" possessed the social prominence Flynn's Sydney associates indicate, neither he nor any agency would have had much difficulty locating her four or five years later. Merely opening a telephone book would have provided her address.

2.  As is so often the case with Errol's autobiography the chronology is simply inadequate. The bejeweled shack-up could not have occurred much before mid-November of 1932. On 30 December our "Diamond Jim" arrived back in Port Moresby on the *Macdhui*, having boarded that vessel in Townsville. Fellow passengers included his pal, Patrol Officer

Jack Hides, who was returning from a holiday visit in Sydney. This allows only a month for well digging, hogget dagging, testicle biting, and all of the other harum-scarum activities which Errol tells us took place in the Queensland back country.

3.  It is true that Vera Giblin, wife of the Port Moresby doctor and Errol's good friend, won lease # 5 in a drawing held on 5 December. But, according to the *Papuan Courier*, she departed for Australia on the *Macdhui* three days later and returned on 9 February. The next day she flew from Port Moresby to Wau to inspect her lease. It is most difficult to see how she could have cabled money to Errol from Port Moresby during these weeks or danced a jig on the wharf at Salamaua on the other side of the island.

What appears to have happened in this. Following theft of the jewels lover boy had to flee. Flight indicates the auburn-haired beauty or her husband did indeed go to the police. Errol took off for the north, perhaps by rail, and eventually booked passage from Townsville to Port Moresby by steamer. As we shall see, he quickly severed his tobacco plantation ties and moved further north to New Guinea. He busied himself there for a few weeks and then disappeared. Errol Flynn's island friends of those days recall he had to get out fast, but none of them were quite sure why. An angry Madge Parks divested of her jewels (diamonds, pearls, or whatever they were) or perhaps an even angrier Mr. Parks divested of god-knows-what provide the answer.

# Chapter Six

## Farewell to the Islands, too!

During the first week of 1933 Errol Flynn ended whatever tenuous connections he had in the Port Moresby area. The *Papuan Courier* of 13 January announced that the Laloki Tobacco Plantation approximately fifteen miles out of town on the "main" road, formerly owned by "Messrs. Adams and Flynn", had been purchased by Miss Beatrice Grimshaw. The editor said the well-known writer planned to hire a European manager for the property and would continue the cultivation of tobacco there.

From the time Flynn leaves Port Moresby on the southern coast of the island of New Guinea until he pops up briefly in Hong Kong a couple of months later his movements are, to say the least, mysterious. However, realizing that the long arm of the Sydney police force might still find him and his very valuable shaving brush, he undoubtedly scurried fast and quietly, perhaps using a false identity at times.

His name does not appear on any passenger lists in either the *Papuan Courier* or the *Rabaul Times*, although H. R. Niall recalls that early in January Flynn disembarked at Salamaua from a steamer on which he was traveling. He says Errol was full of grandiose schemes for starting a gold syndicate of some sort; but, Niall adds, "Nobody would put up any money, so he went on to Rabaul". Several other island residents of that era are able to provide additional clues to Flynn's whereabouts, and a unique journal discovered two years later even records some of the thoughts of the man himself during these weeks.

In August of 1935 Mr. and Mrs. Allan Innes decided to sell their interests on the isthmus of Salamaua and move to Sydney.

By that date their hotel with its store, ice-making plant, and subsidiary facilities had become a landmark of considerable importance. It was the last stop for miners heading into the gold fields and the first on the way out. Innes hospitality was legion throughout the islands. In addition to a myriad of services, this couple also stored goods which travelers and miners lodged with them from time to time. Faced with high freight rates it was not unusual for a man heading inland for six months or more to pack a tea chest or trunk with belongings he did not need, seal it up (perhaps with a padlock), and scrawl his name on one end. These boxes, with the names clearly visible, were then stacked in a loft in a shed.

As Innes prepared to leave he was confronted with the problem of numerous boxes and trunks whose owners had failed to return to pick up their property. Not knowing quite what to do, he called in the district officer who watched as the containers were opened. He took whatever might have legal significance; the remainder was thrown away or given to the natives. One of these boxes had "Errol Flynn" written on it. Inside Innes found a few personal belongings of no special value and a collection of sheets and towels appropriated from the Hotel Salamaua! Nestled within the linen lay a Croxley "exercise book", a type familiar to any Australian schoolboy of the 1930s, but cut neatly in half so as to fit a man's pocket. It turned out to be a record of business notes, scraps of a diary, and random comments written by Flynn in January of 1933.

At the time of this discovery the name of "Errol Flynn" was to say the least, not well-known. He had arrived in Hollywood from England only a few months before and had been cast in two undistinguished productions. Neither effort provided much opportunity for flair, bravado, and dashing sword play. In *The Case of the Curious Bride*, a Perry Mason thriller, the handsome lad from Hobart was seen for only a minute or two—once as a corpse and later in a flashback in which he had no dialogue. However, this inauspicious beginning introduced him to Michael Curtiz who would direct most of his super-successful swashbucklers during the next two decades. *Don't Bet on Blondes* let Errol appear for about five minutes as a society playboy in love with Guy Kibbee's daughter. Although he did not get the girl, the role was, of course, a natural vehicle for Flynn charm and ego and one for which he had considerable background experience.

In mid-1935, about the time that the Inneses found his notebook, these brief experiences before American cameras won Flynn the title role in *Captain Blood,* a tale of England, Jamaica, and slavery at the time of the Glorious Revolution of 1688-9 and the movie which catapulted him to stardom. Rafael Sabatini's novel, made into a silent film in the 1920s, had been re-issued by a Sydney publishing house, Angus and Robertson, during Flynn's New Guinea years. In April of 1931 the *Papuan Courier* printed a lengthy, laudatory review which Errol possibly may have read or perhaps it even encouraged him to secure a copy of this classic.

According to the three young man who compiled *The Films of Errol Flynn*, Warner Brothers decided to re-make this epic because of the obvious success of historical adventures during the depths of the depression, a form of escapism which won worldwide favour. Robert Donat, who had played the Count of Monte Cristo, was the leading contender for the role of Captain Peter Blood, but due to contract difficulties he was not available. Having committed themselves to production, the studio needed a leading man at once. "It was", in the opinion of these authors, "a question of the right man being in the right place at the right time." *Captain Blood* also gave star status to another young stage hopeful, Olivia de Havilland.

Thomas, Behlmer, and McCarty devote seven pages to this epic, so clearly a turning point in Errol Flynn's career, and have these comments concerning the results.

Flynn, considering his limited acting experience, did an exceptional job. It was wide-open gallantry, but the fervor was nicely tempered with utter sincerity and a somewhat impudent charm, thereby laying the groundwork for the essential Flynn acting style. His pairing with the young, pert, and lovely de Havilland seemed to produce the right screen chemistry.

Flynn was quite nervous during the first days of shooting, and his performance reflected this. As he gained confidence, his acting improved considerably; so much so that later on the first two weeks' footage was filmed again.

During the shooting of one of the action scenes on board the ship, Flynn collapsed from a recurrence of malaria, originally contracted by the actor in New Guinea.

'Captain Blood' opened in December, 1935 (six weeks following 'Mutiny on the Bounty'), to generally excellent reviews. The public took to the film, Flynn, and de Havilland immediately. Swashbucklers—old-fashioned 'moving' pictures—were once again in, and Warners had the only first-rate swashbuckler to handle the assignments.

These authors note that today the film looks somewhat "dated", yet remains worthy of consideration on several counts: it was Errol's first swashbuckler and the genesis of the Flynn image; his first starring role; the first of several very successful appearances with Olivia de Havilland; the first film scored by the noted Austrian composer Erich Wolfgang Korngold; and Flynn's first major assignment under the direction of Michael Curtiz who would work with him in eight subsequent productions. The success of *Captain Blood*, which Warner Brothers put together as unexpensively as possible, convinced studio heads that now they could spend real money on their new star—the former tobacco grower, labor recruiter, plantation overseer, air cargo clerk, grease monkey, and general roustabout of New Guinea, New Britain, and Papua.

All of these dramatic developments in Hollywood were unknown to Mrs. Allen Innes half a world away on the tiny isthmus of Salamaua. As she and her husband packed their belongings for shipment to Sydney, they had to decide what to do with the grubby little notebook they had found stored with their stolen linen. For various reasons, none of them influenced by Errol Flynn the movie star for that he was not in mid-1935, she concluded the best thing to do was to keep the diary. "It wasn't mine to destroy", Mrs. Innes observed, "and there were some notes in it he may have wanted to keep. Also, he might have come back."

In the late 1930s, while visiting in America, she tried to return the notebook to its rightful owner, but got nowhere. The star's staff would not let her see him. During succeeding decades a handful of articles based upon this diary have been published. The most authoritative of these is Stuart Inder's "His Wicked, Wicked Ways" which appeared in the *Pacific Islands Monthly* of November 1960, obviously inspired by the autobiography which was then a best-seller. An adaptation of that article was featured in an Australian weekly, *People* (18 January, 1961).

In the years since 1935 original material found in the notebook unfortunately has undergone some alteration. One might call this censorship; but, it if is, the reasons for it are understandable enough. Mrs. Innes, very ill and unable to contact Flynn, was afraid the diary might fall into unscrupulous hands . . . so, she decided to destroy some of what she calls the "purple" passages in which Errol Flynn named names and boasted of his sexual successes in New Guinea. Nevertheless, what remains is a fascinating record of the future movie star's activities and thoughts early in 1933. Perhaps even more fascinating is the possibility that this diary is yet another Flynn fabrication—but, first to what is left of this strange document.

Flynn begins these notes while at Sattelberg Lutheran Mission about six and one-half miles from Finschhafen on New Guinea's northern coast. Finschhafen, scene of very bitter fighting during World War II, lies at the end of the Huon Peninsula some seventy miles east of the Lae-Salamaua area.

It is mid-January and he is recruiting native labor. Before the week described comes to an end, Flynn moves on to Fior, a small village a few miles north of the mission station. Some explanatory material has been inserted in brackets and obvious spelling errors corrected—Finschhafen for "Finchhafen", Sattelberg for "Saddleberg", Fior for "Fio" . . . but, except for the deletions made by Mrs. Innes, the diary and comments remain essentially as found amid Hotel Salamaua linen in 1935.

Sattelberg Mission—13th Jan., 1933.

> Arrived here at 5 p.m. after leaving Finschhafen this morning at 10 a.m. Broke journey half way at Yermen to give my boys time to cook some rice. Carriers would not carry beyond Yermen so paid them off and sent to Yehu for a new lot. Cost of carrying very high in this district—they all know what money is. Sattelberg is 3650 ft. above sea level but commands wonderful outlook over the sea—I can see Umboi Island from here—it must be 80 miles away.
>
> Queer lot these Lutheran missionaries. For the main part they are Germans but there is a sprinkling of Australians of German parentage. Father Helbig [a lay helper, one of six people at the mission] met me and gave me this room—very comfortable and I 'm dog weary and a bit footsore as is usual on the first day out.
>
> Coloured prints of Christ are regarding me dolefully from every angle in the room. He is portrayed in a large variety of postures. Rebuking (or confusing) the Elders who have the longest & whitest beards I've ever seen; conferring blessings, etc. Why is it that Christ is never shown smiling? He must have laughed sometimes. The prints are old though, probably done some 20 or 30

years ago when gaiety of any sort was still regarded as sinful.

Sattelberg Mission is the health resort for run-down & enervated missionaries. They're sent up here for a month every year to get the benefit of the excellent climate. I spotted a pretty girl when I came in today so I'll have to shave tonight. Three days growth is no good even for a recruiter to wear. She's the little Dutch sister, I suppose—hope she comes to the table to-night. [There were three lady helpers at the mission, all unmarried: Clara Helbig, Jutta Keysser, and Marie Uke.]

These missionaries treat their women folk like dirt. I stood up last night when Karchner's wife came into the room at Finschhafen and only succeeded in embarrassing everyone present!!! It was a quite unprecedented occurrence for the entrance of a woman to be more than curtly acknowledged by a sort of grunt. The idea is for all the men to sit down and eat what the women bring in at odd intervals. When in Rome do as the Dagoes do, thenceforth I kept my seat and grunted.

They sing grace in German before every meal. I very nearly laughed aloud last night at a young Bavarian, newly arrived in the country, who was making the bravest effort to lower the tone of his naturally high falsetto voice. He had fully a dozen hairs in his beard.

Long day's march tomorrow—hope to make the Hube country in four days from here. If the rain holds off may make it in three. If it doesn't I won't be able to cross the Waria River, perhaps for a week. Thank God I brought 2 bottles of O. P. rum and the Bible, and will thus have both drink and something to read. Have often wanted to read the Bible—I believe it's very entertaining & instructive. There goes the kai-kai [dinner] bell. Hungry lot these missionaries, so I'd better get along or the board will be cleared.

14th

Stayed at Sattelberg today and rearranged my equipment for cheaper carrying. The paramount luluai of the District Selembe came up to see me this evening. We had a long discussion, with Wasange and Tutuman, the two tultuls, being present. [A luluai was a headman or chief confirmed by the territorial administration; a tultul was a native government official and interpreter in a village.] The old man is a very distinct personality, quite a superior type. He has agreed to help me recruit after, no doubt, making extensive inquiries about me from my own boys, summing me up by the text of our talk and the added incentive of Kyle's message brought by Tutuman. He has agreed to send out three tultuls in different directions—Tutuman to go to the Waria River, Inge to go to Mape, and Sambar to the beginning of the Hube country. They will meet me at Fior Village in four days time (Saturday).

Fior, Wednesday 15th.

Left Sattelberg after lunch at 2 p.m. and arrived at Fior at 4:30. The track is about the best I have found inland and very beautiful besides. Crossed three mountain streams, each one dammed up at the crossing into crystal clear pools. Bathed in the last one; first bath in three days. These pellucid pools were typical of New Guinea's specious beauty. They were fed by a sparkling stream flowing over bright limestone and fringed by capiac palms and coconuts. Several varieties of orchids were flowering among the surrounding undergrowth.

I sent the carriers on ahead & shedding singlet & shorts leapt joyously into the cold water and lay there, lazily enjoying the rare sensation of a plunge bath and admiring my surroundings. As I lay there idly floating I noticed what I took to be innumerable small black twigs attaching themselves one by one to my body, but took little notice of them. Then horrible thoughts occurred to me. I jumped up hurriedly and found my fears realized. I was covered in leeches who obviously hadn't had a square meal in months.

Luckily I had matches with me so spent an hour burning them off, a proceeding which was watched with keen interest by some 10 boys who had come back along the track to find me. If leeches are removed by any other method except burning their tails to make them release their hold, a tropical ulcer will almost invariably form on the spot. I now look like a leopard, after dabbing myself with iodine on the bites.

Thursday, 16th, Fior Village.

The mission has obviously benefited these people greatly in a number of ways. They have good roads, 20 odd head of cattle bought from the mission and bred up from an original three or four head. I know of no other natives who own a herd of cattle. They also grow English potatoes, kohlrabi, tomatoes. This morning I bought 24 green corn cobs, a dozen or so taroes for 1/-; a pineapple & half a dozen cucumbers were thrown into the bargain.

I think Wasange will get me a recruit here.

There is a little stream running right through this village and the rest house is situated a hundred yards or so from the village. Consequently I have no giant & irrepressible native pigs & dogs to annoy me. I thought at first I might get a little privacy too, but that is expecting too much. My every action has been keenly observed by at least 50 pairs of eyes ever since I arrived. But I'm very comfortable here and waiting until Saturday is not going to be so bad as I thought, particularly as corn, eggs, & fruit are plentiful & of course very cheap.

Was very amused last night. My three Aitape boys, being in a strange country and having been used to finding enemies if they strayed a yard beyond their own hunting grounds in Wapi, have been scared stiff ever since they left the coast. An old woman brought them some taro last night. Although very hungry they examined it dubiously & then asked Wasange, who was sitting down outside their house, 'Are you sure this food is not poisoned?'

Wasange couldn't understand what they were asking at first & they had to repeat the question several times. When he did, he and the entire gathering burst out laughing at my 'bushmen'. With good cause, of course, as I suppose this village has been peaceful for 10 years or so. But it was not a ridiculous question. After all, only two days march further in, and the Hube, they would not stop at a small thing like poison if they thought there was something to be gained from it.

I hear there is some trouble in Hube over a woman. Two villages are about to fight, so the talk goes. If it's right, things couldn't be better for me. Am bound to get recruits, probably from both villages if there's a fight as they'll want to get away to escape reprisals later.

17th, Fior Village.

First boy this morning—good stamp of native, too. He'll look well leading an axe about although he doesn't suspect it yet. He thinks he's going to be my cook. This is a very good omen—to get a boy from the chief's village means that I'll almost certainly get as many as I want from other villages.

Big 'talk-talk' last night. The chief and his two tultuls came along and we discussed everything under the sun including the late war which appears to cause much amusement and astonishment. That all the white men should indulge in extensive fighting among themselves after having given them, the black men, the very strictest injunctions against fighting, with prompt & severe punishment for disobedience, must, I suppose, appear to them somewhat paradoxical. It must have chafed them a bit when they heard details of the Great War and were themselves prevented from carrying out those periodical raids & sorties against the neighbouring villages which used to be their favorite occupation & hobby before we came along and told them they had to be friends.

18th, Fior.

Two more boys making three now. Excellent going. Went down to the Bun River yesterday—very peculiar formation, mainly a sort of limestone bottom with no wash in the river bed to speak of at all. Good looking wash on both banks though with no overburden more than 2 or 3 feet at any part. Will wash a few dishes down there tomorrow although it's very unlikely if there's even colours. I believe all these rivers were well prospected years ago by the German missionaries & others.

Have just finished reading *The Good Companions*. Wonderful. Can Priestley ask for anything more from life than that gift of expression? I felt I knew personally every one of those characters at the end. Especially Micham Moreton—if he had been drawn from old Simpson, ex-actor-manager now sandalwood king of Papua, he couldn't have been described more faithfully.

Three more boys tonight.

19th, Fior.

The rush has set in properly. Tutuman came back with 7 boys which makes 13 and I'll have two more tomorrow.

As all my boys come from the purlieus of this district all the old men of Fior decided to read me an address. It was rather amusing. The entire village gathered round me while I sat in the middle of the circle on a tucker box. One old grey beard then got to his feet and began to harangue me in forcible but quite incomprehensible terms as he spoke in his own language.

I however nodded solemnly at each pause and later had his speech interpreted. He said in effect that Fior had given me all their young men and I must look after them well. He enjoined me that I must not sell any of them & when their time had finished must bring them back myself and then I would be given new boys to take their place. He then wound up by stating that although he was talking to me in strong words I must not think he was 'cross'—and when I came would I bring him a dog? He then asked me, through the interpreter, if I would shake hands with him and I did.

20th, Fior.

Broke camp this morning having recruited 16 boys (with my 3 Aitapes makes 19) and proceeded.
At this point Errol Flynn's diary ends, but the notes continue with a series of haphazard quotations, lists of boys recruited, and some random observations . . . some of them quite revealing. First there is his recollection of John Masefield's "Sea-Fever", a poem also reproduced in *Beam Ends*.

> I must go down to the sea again
> To the rolling sea & the sky
> For all I ask is a tall ship
> And the wheels kick & the brown spume & the
>     white sail's shaking,
> And a gray mist on the sea's face & a grey dawn
>     breaking.
>
> I must go down to the sea again
> To the gulls way and the whale's way
> Where the wind's like a whetted knife
> And a merry tale from a laughing fellow rover
> & quiet sleep & a sweet dream when the long trick's over.

Any Masefield fan can quickly pick holes in Errol's version. Lines are missing and many words are incorrect. But, perhaps this effort is about as accurate as many of us might piece together if asked to do so from memory. This excerpt is followed by the names of native recruits or assistants and goods and clothing issued to each. For example, "Tirmbong, Ningio, Dome—lap lap & singlet; Homé (tultul)—striped costume, serge lap lap, boy's blouse, salt; Kane—beads; Bonieve—lap lap . . ." Then there is a native poem or song, perhaps to balance the misquoted work of Masefield.

Before me boy belong Companee
He grease im along fuse
Now me catchim big fella trouble
Now me stop calaboose.

Fashion belong me e good fella fashion
Me no savvy laze
By'm by me loose in calaboose
My Christ me go quick a long place!
O calaboose e no 1 place.

This is apparently a jailhouse (calaboose) lament by a company boy gone wrong. Someone persuaded him (in pidgin "girisim" may mean persuade, cajole, etc.) to steal a "fuse" of coins—perhaps shillings since it was customary for banks to prepare them for customers in wrapped rolls. His fashion ("feshin" means habit, custom, manner) is honest, hard work—"me no savvy laze". And when he's free he'll get as far as possible from the jail as soon as he can—"My Christ me go quick a long place".

Then a group of disjointed sentences appear: "The time I passed Dusty Miller on a lorry in Madang with 11 boys for recruiting trip. He saw me when I waved, turned around and went into the house. Bill Stower and the egg trick on L.

Bennett's Mary's head." Miller, Flynn's recruiting buddy of the late 1920s, later married Lillian Bennett ("Tiger Lil"). He died in Sydney in 1959, the same year that Flynn succumbed to a sudden heart attack in British Columbia. Mary, usually spelled "meri", is the pidgin word for a native woman, any white woman being called "misis". In some parts of New Guinea one can still see public toilets marked "meri".

Those brief, inconclusive comments are followed by a series of notes, some for business and some for pleasure. It would seem that Errol Flynn, always interested in a writing career, was jotting down thoughts which someday might become essays or articles.

> Marco Polo always recorded his surprise when he found no olives in the strange places he visited. The Chinese also betrayed astonishment when they learned the West had no bamboo—a lack which seemed to them incredible. So, also, of all the wonders of our modern civilization nothing astounds a New Guinea native more than the fact that there are no coconuts growing in the lands whence we white men come. They cannot imagine a coconutless existence for to them the tree is the mainstay of life and supplies them with all their major necessities—food, clothing, house-building material, as well as countless other uses.

> Essay on Several 'Don'ts' in 'The Art
> & Niceties of Seduction' (without trousers)

Compromising positions to avoid—Avenues of escape must be arranged first. Avoid betraying astonishment at credulity of victim—even in the dark. Draw analogy between the mention of word 'marriage' & he who uses dynamite in exasperation after having failed with dry fly. Use of alcohol is to be deprecated except as a last resort.

After these intriguing excerpts comes another list of recruits, showing their names, amount of money paid each one, his home village, luluai, and nearest relative. This list continues for three and one-half pages. Then Flynn reflects upon his immediate future, lists another group of boys, and concludes with a mundane summary of supplies he must get: "tin opener, mustard, writing pad, lock & key, rucksack, toilet paper, and frying pan". But, to his very revealing introspection:

> I am going to China because I wish to live deliberately. New Guinea offers me, it is true, satisfaction for the tastes I have acquired which only leisure can satisfy. I am leaving economic security and I am leaving it deliberately. By going off to China with a paltry few pounds and no knowledge of what life has in store for me there I believe that I am going to front the essentials of life to see if I can learn what it has to teach and above all not to discover when I come to die, that I have not lived.
>
> We fritter our lives away in detail, but I am not going to do this. I am going to live deeply, to acknowledge not one of the so-called social forces which hold our lives in thrall & reduce us to economic dependency. The best part of life is spent in earning money in order to enjoy a questionable liberty during the least valuable part of it. To hell with money! Pursuit of it is not going to mould my life for me. I am going to live sturdily & Spartan-like, to drive life into a corner & reduce it to its lowest terms and if I find it sublime I shall know it by experience—and not make wistful conjectures about it conjured up by illustrated magazines. I refuse to accept the ideology of a business world which believes that man at hard labour is the noblest work of God. Leisure to use as I see fit!

One can never become a skillful reader or acquire the ability to appreciate books, unless one first cultivates a keen sense of the relative value of things; for this sense is the quintessence of true education & culture. To learn what is worth one's while is the largest part of the Art of Life.

Time, for example, just one hour of time is far more important than money for time is life. Whenever you waste your time over printed words that neither enlighten or amuse you, you are, in a sense, committing suicide. The value, the intrinsic value, of our actions, emotions, thoughts, possessions, way of life, occupations, of the manner in which we are living—this is the first thing to be determined; for unless we are *satisfied* that any of these things have a true value, even if only relative, our lives are futile, and there is no more hopeless realization than this.

Now there are several things wrong with these pencilled notes found at Salamaua in 1935. The most obvious is that Errol Flynn had no intention whatsoever of living and working in China. The few weeks spent before the camera at Bondi Junction had fired his imagination. Perhaps *this* was the route to quick riches—despite his cry of "To hell with money!" Elsa Chauvel says her husband immediately sensed the theatrical flair which Flynn possessed and advised him to get to England as fast as possible. There he might get the training and experience necessary for a film or stage career.

Sydney associates recall that the Cinesound staff made up a substantial number of publicity photos for the star of *In the Wake of the Bounty*. Seen in this light, his high praise bestowed upon Priestley's *The Good Companions* is especially interesting for that novel describes the adventures of a traveling English stage company. However, once more as with Masefield's "Sea-Fever", Flynn's memory falters. The Priestley character he refers to is Morton Mitcham, not "Micham Moreton".

A few islands associates knew this young man's true goal was England, not China. J. K. McCarthy writes in *Patrol Into Yesterday: My New Guinea Years* (Melbourne, 1963) of an encounter with Errol early in 1933 in Salamaua. McCarthy, who had known him in Kokopo during his weeks as a cadet, says he was as debonair and as charming as ever but flat broke and adds that he owed money to several miners who in their generosity had advanced him substantial sums. These private debts were no concern of McCarthy, a district officer; but, when a group of natives came seeking help in securing wages Flynn owned them, the future movie star's indebtedness became a government matter. Despite his troubles, McCarthy found him extremely optimistic.

> 'You don't have to worry about a thing,' he said. 'I am just waiting on some money that's owed me in Australia. And there are a few cheques due locally in a day or two. By the way, I suppose you've heard of Elstree Studios in England? I've been offered a contract—cash in advance—and I'm thinking of accepting.
>
> I kept after Errol for several days. He was charming, and his optimism unbounded. Finally he paid up—to my surprise, although he didn't owe the natives much. He owed Weine and the others much more, with the result that when, shortly after this incident, Errol Flynn suddenly left New Guinea, the things that were being said about him in Salamaua were far from complimentary.

The offer from Elstree Studios sounds like another bit of Flynn blarney. Since his only movie had not yet been screened before an audience, any "cash in advance" offer from faraway England is highly unlikely. But the boast of checks "about to appear" has a familiar ring to it. The Will Jeffersons, his reluctant hosts at Ogamobu rubber plantation at Kikori, heard the same tale over and over in May of 1932. Of course, we know Errol Flynn was not broke, nor was he "deliberately" leaving "economic security" and going off with "a paltry few pounds". Passage from Rabaul to Hong Kong to London was not dirt cheap, even in 1933.

Ben Parer, who spent an evening drinking with Flynn during these weeks, remembers he was far from destitute. In his delightfully blunt Aussie brogue, Parer, now a devout member of Alcoholics Anonymous, sketches this portrait of Errol.

> You can tell the shifty-eyed blokes who can't shout their turn at the bar. They sorta hunch up their shoulders and try to become inconspicuous as the bottles empty one by one. Not Flynny-boy! No, sir, not on your life! By God, he was right in there buying his share with the very best of 'em.

Comparison of the material found in his notebook with map and calendar raises more questions. Errol seems to have confused the community of Wareo, a few miles north of Sattelberg Mission, which has no river by that name, with Waria some twenty or thirty miles to the south on the Waria River. And Fior's nearest river is called the Busim or Song, not the "Bun". A New Guinea resident familiar with this region in back of Finschhafen undoubtedly could pinpoint additional errors. But perhaps the most perplexing feature is Errol Flynn's designation of 15 January as "Wednesday" when, in fact, it fell on Sunday! Certainly anyone in the bush can lose track of the days after a month or so . . . but, in a week? That is very difficult to conceive. Also, he was near a mission station much of the time which adhered closely to the calendar and celebrated each Sabbath in an established fashion.

It appears, then, that this journal—clearly written in Errol Flynn's hand—is, like so many of this young man's records, somewhat true and somewhat false. He probably did have experience recruiting labor in the mountainous area he describes, and (as we'll see shortly) there is a possibility he was actually doing so in January of 1933. Storing Hotel Salamaua linen with Mr. and Mrs. Allen Innes, the owners of those sheets and towels, makes little sense. There was virtually no chance that he would return, especially in view of his troubles with "Madge Parks". But, lodging a few items with Allen Innes, writing his name boldly on the box, sealing that box with a lock (one of the things he planned to buy according to his notebook), and enclosing a journal telling any pursuer precisely where he was *not* going smells like yet another bit of Flynniana. The flourishes about his penniless condition and serious contemplation of a Chinese career are particularly suspect.

If nothing else, these pages bear remarkable similarity to the novel, *Showdown*, published in 1946. After a bout with blackwater fever, the hero, beautiful young Shamus O'Thames, captain of the schooner *Maski*, is nursed back to health by a Lutheran missionary, Father Kirshner (Karchner?). The locale is New Guinea's northern coast, and the mission staff includes one lovely young girl, Sister Ganice, whom Shamus loves from afar. ("I spotted a pretty girl as I came in today so I'll have to shave tonight.")

Flynn's autobiography contains random snatches of this recruiting tale; but, once more, it is of little help. He has "Finchhafen" south of Salamaua, the missionaries are Catholic, and after bamboozling a village chief with a coin trick (making shillings out of San Francisco fair tokens with the aid of quicksilver) he gets a fine harvest of boys. He takes those lads to Salamaua whose hardened recruiters are amazed by such good fortune. Errol then makes a quick trip to the gold fields where he has limited success at the joint Flynn-Giblin lease.

According to Dr. Dexter Giblin, this Edie Creek venture was a bizarre undertaking from the outset. Sometime in mid-1932 shortly before Errol sailed for Sydney, he and Trelawney Adams were having morning tea with Giblin's parents. Conversation turned to the sale of tickets in a drawing for several gold leases, and the four friends resolved that each would buy one. If any of them was lucky, then each would have a one-fourth interest. No papers were drawn up. This was simply a good-natured, oral agreement which might have been forgotten had Vera Giblin not won lease # 5 at the drawing held on 5 December.

As mentioned earlier, three days later Mrs. Giblin left Port Moresby for Sydney and did not return until 9 February. Errol, as we know, was adrift somewhere between Sydney and Townsville dagging sheep and drilling wells, station owners' teenage daughters, etc. He arrived back in Port Moresby on 30 December but soon closed out his tobacco interests and sailed on to Salamaua. It appears that talk of "a gold syndicate" which H. R. Niall heard when he met Flynn on the boat taking them around to New Guinea's north coast was inspired by word from Vera Giblin in Australia. Since Errol had a one-fourth interest in the Edie Creek lease and was footloose and out of work, she apparently asked him to recruit some boys and begin digging "their" fortune at once. If this did happen it helps to explain Flynn's presence at Sattelberg in mid-January.

However, the future film idol did not tarry long in New Guinea. The last entry in his journal-diary is dated 20 January, and one month later he was on New Britain, several hundred miles away. This means Flynn had to walk from Fior to Finschhafen, sail down the coast to either Salamaua or Lae, hike up to Edie Creek with boys (or perhaps they flew in), return to the coast, and sail to Rabaul. If he did not use aircraft during part of these travels he clearly was on the move most of the time, trudging through some of the roughest terrain in the world.

Since Mrs. Giblin visited Edie Creek on 10 February, we can assume Errol was there then. Thus, after countless diversions and innumerable digressions, the good-looking youth from Hobart was at last a real, live miner. He was bossing some twenty to thirty boys, and the future looked bright indeed. The owner of a nearby lease had already shipped more than 40,000 ounces of gold south to Sydney.

Yet, having achieved his goal of the past five years, Flynn suddenly abandoned Edie Creek after only a few days. He tells us in *My Wicked, Wicked Ways* that he concluded it was time to leave New Guinea. He feared among other things, he says, that the bilked luluai would come yelling to the government with the fair tokens and cause him considerable trouble. So he sold his boys, signed his share of the Edie Creek lease over to a Townsville railway man who had befriended him during his Queensland jaunt (why not to "Madge" who "befriended" him earlier and much, much more?), and made his way to Rabaul.

Dr. Dexter Giblin says his mother had placed great faith in Errol Flynn, even giving him power of attorney over their lease. It was she who paid for the recruiting tour, and the contracts of the boys obtained in the Fior area actually were not Flynn's to sell. However, Vera Giblin did not bear her wayward associate any ill will at all. Her son recalls that she merely shrugged philosophically, noting that it actually was Errol who did the hard work of securing the natives. Mrs. Giblin also emphasized that she was among the first urging Flynn to seek out a stage career. If some of her money helped him get to London, he went with her blessing.

Some New Guinea friends say he stole away quietly. As McCarthy noted, Flynn owed several hundred pounds to a variety of people in the Wau-Salamaua area; and, if any creditor thought a debtor was about to skip out of the territory, all he had to do was alert Burns Philp. That company, which controlled all regular steamer service, would refuse passage until settlement of debts was arranged. So Errol apparently spread the story of yet another recruiting trip and then slipped out to New Britain on a small schooner, perhaps one operated by his pal, Trelawney Adams.

"Tiger Lil", however, remember a going-away party held in Flynn's honor. She also recalls a hilarious seduction scene which misfired. This is how it happened. Errol went calling late one evening upon a young married lady of Salamaua. Her husband was not at home, she had already retired, but they were old friends and he said all he wanted to do was have a chat. His hostess returned to bed, Flynn poured each of them a drink, and they relaxed over casual conversation . . . but, before long, our friend was up to his usual tricks. In the midst of this amorous horseplay Errol suddenly cried out in pain, leapt from the bed, seized his ankle, and undoubtedly uttered some emotion charged phrases. It seems the lady's meri (native maid) was sleeping under the bed. Sensing that something was not quite right above her, she reached out and sank her teeth into Flynn's skin. Thus ended the romantic interlude.

On the eve of his departure from the islands Flynn says he made some unusual but very lucrative business transactions at Rabaul. He shipped fifty ounces of Edie Creek gold to England via a branch of Barclay's Bank and bought still more diamonds from a dockside "IDB"—an illicit diamond buyer. The *Pacific Islands Monthly's* review of *My Wicked, Wicked Ways* found this episode especially ridiculous, terming (somewhat unfairly) the entire New Guinea sequence "largely piffle". Anyway, Errol tells us how a short time later he boarded a "dowdy freighter" and watched as the hills of New Britain, "green and fresh as ever", receded in the distance.

There is a better than fifty-fifty chance our stalwart young stud sailed on the *Nankin*, an Eastern and Australian Steamship Company boat, which left Rabaul on 21 February. The *Nankin*, a freighter which also took passengers, got to Manila on 1 March and arrived in Hong Kong on 4 March. His cabin mates included two German brothers named Konke. They were carpenters who had gone north with read-cut dormitories which Allen Innes ordered from Brisbane. After the task of adding those structures to the Hotel Salamaua was completed they had worked in Lae for several months.

According to the Konkes, when they arrived at Hong Kong Errol picked up a small package he had lodged with the purser. A short time later he declared it had been tampered with and some diamonds were missing. Police were called in, and the Konkes, much to their consternation, were grilled for hours. Some individuals think the steamship company made a settlement of some sort with Flynn; others say nothing was decided. Instead, the authorities asked Errol and those involved to report to police headquarters the next day. Flynn never showed up, having left immediately for England. The latter story, as we shall see shortly, seems much more plausible.

As usual, *My Wicked, Wicked Ways* contains fragments of this tale, but "Part Three: Seven Seas to England, 1932-1933", is probably the most fanciful section of the entire book. It describes a rollicking, rip-roaring, eight-month, whorehousing trip from Rabaul to London. There are wild times in Manila, Hong Kong, Macao, Shanghai, Saigon, Ceylon, Calcutta, Djibouti, Addis Ababa, Marseilles, etc., plus a short stint in the Royal Hong Kong Volunteers . . . service in which Flynn took considerable pride and always cited in his *Who's Who* entries. As for his diamond collection, he says it was stolen in Hong Kong, hence all of the turmoil and numerous digressions *en route* to England.

O. K. Let's backtrack a bit. It is obvious Flynn departed from the islands early in 1933, not 1932. And, by the way, he left his huge Alsatian dog with relatives of Mr. and Mrs. Innes amid fervent promises to return shortly and pick up the animal. If he traveled on the *Nankin* from Rabaul (and he probably did), there was no opportunity for the Philippine playtime which he describes in glorious, full-blown phrases, and the Hong Kong sequences are also 99 per cent fiction. On 30 September, 1971, in answer to a query, Lieutenant Colonel J. Chapman, commanding officer of the Hong Kong Regiment (formerly the Volunteers . . . motto "Nulli Secundus in Oriente"), wrote me the following letter:

> We have searched through our records of the 1930s and can find no trace of Errol Leslie Thomson Flynn ever

having been a member of the Hong Kong Volunteer Defence Corps (as it was called in those days). We have also asked those who were Volunteers in those days and no one remembers him. Had he been a Volunteer at any stage he would certainly be talked of—his type of films has always been very popular locally.

In addition, Flynn's autobiography quotes a letter written to his father from Colombo, Ceylon, in March of 1933. It tells how he and a traveling buddy, a gigantic German doctor named Gerrit H. Koets, escaped the horrors of the Sino-Japanese War by producing Chinese laundry slips which were accepted as passports! Well, admittedly it makes a fine story and is clearly in the Flynn tradition. This man Koets may have been the elusive Herman F. Erben, alias "Joel Swartz".

Once in merrie England Flynn's career began in earnest, and within a year or so he was able to push himself into movies once more. Although one cannot call his performances breath-taking, luck was with him. Irving Asher of Warner Brothers was looking for "British" types to export to Hollywood. His wife saw Errol waiting in her husband's outer office and immediately told him to give that handsome youth special consideration. According to *The Films of Errol Flynn*, Asher put Flynn under contract without seeing him on the screen or waiting for the usual testing procedures. In October of 1934 he cabled his bosses in Burbank:

> Signed today seven years' optional contract best picture bet we have ever seen. He twenty-five Irish looks cross between Charles Farrell and George Brent same type and build excellent actor champion boxer swimmer guarantee he real find.

We know Errol Flynn wasn't Irish nor was he a champion swimmer or boxer—but he was good looking, of superior build, and "a real find", even if not an "excellent" actor. Seventy-two hours later, for reasons best known to Asher, Flynn was given the lead in *Murder at Monte Carlo*, a British production.

Soon he was crossing the Atlantic on his way to America, Hollywood, and fame. On the liner he met Lili Damita, then an established screen personality, who later became the first of his three wives. (A Dalgety associate recalls that Errol was enamored with Lili back in Sydney in 1927.)

According to rumor, Warner Brothers knew something of this young man's flamboyant, footloose ways and, when he arrived in New York City, presented him with a minimum of spending money and a one-way ticket to the West Coast, nothing more. Errol boarded the transcontinental flyer and promptly disappeared. Some days later employees of the studio found his shacked up in Chicago. For reasons of his own Flynn had decided to cash in the remainder of his ticket and test the reputed joys of the Windy City.

New Guinea, Sydney, Hobart, and all of the associations with those regions were now history, and Warner Brothers, eager to exploit their "British" find, for the time being played down any references to that corner of the world. The new star was "Irish", a change of nationality which delighted Flynn who had always yearned to be accepted as a product of the British Isles. With his parents now living in Belfast and a name like Flynn it all made sense. Once he became an established swashbuckler, however, more and more of his exotic tropical background was permitted to filter into print.

By the 1950s Errol would even re-discover his Tasmanian origins and take considerable pride in a Hobart boyhood. He once greeted an Australian reporter in Manhattan with a fast query as to whether or not he might be Tasmanian. Disappointed, Flynn vowed he would meet someone from his island homeland someday soon and then launched into a description of how he remembered (as a lad of twelve or so) watching firm little female behinds as they joggled from side to side up the steep hills of Hobart.

American publicity agents were so successful that, although they too subsequently aired elements of this star's colourful past, thousands of fans accepted him as a product of Erin's old sod. As his career prospered and reached tempestuous heights Australians were quite willing to let the Irish have the "Tasmanian Devil" as their very own. Comment in the *Pacific Islands Monthly* during the 1930s reflects this view—at first genuine pride in the local boy who is making it big on the silver screen . . . then some derision and scorn followed by silence. This journal, by the way, is printed in Sydney using material collected from the islands throughout the southwestern Pacific.

In January of 1937, a year or so after Errol Flynn achieved star status, the *Monthly* announced that he planned to return to his copra plantation, settle down, and never go back to the bright lights of Hollywood. The editor failed to say just where that plantation might be located, but five months later he was more specific concerning the former tobacco fields near Port Moresby. He said the bungalow on the property near Laloki was falling into decay and added that folks in both Moresby and Wau told many funny stores about Flynn.

> He was a doughty and usually victorious fighter, and some of the young bloods of 'Port' now seem inclined to boast of the rather terrific hidings they received at his hands.

A year later this journal said that Errol had written a song entitled "Tahiti Lullayb" for *The Singing Cop*, a movie to be made in the South Seas, and it reported in October 1938 that the star was suffering from a recurrence of malaria. A Honolulu item (11 April, 1939) noting that the new *Sirocco* was being detained because aliens could not own large vessels earned this comment from the *Monthly's* editor: "This is something which our old friend may not be able to talk himself out of". (Flynn became a U.S. citizen in 1942.)

In September 1940 the *Monthly* passed a much more severe judgment. A two-page article containing a hefty helping of public relations blather ended with this observation:

> The stories make lovely 'copy' for thrill-hungry
> shop-girls and their boy-friends; but quite a number of
> Islands people who knew the irrepressible Errol in the
> Territories are more than ever convinced that bluff old
> Barnum was right.

Like Australians and Tasmanians, residents of New Guinea
had decided that if the Irish wanted him, by God, they could
have him!

And all evidence indicates the feeling was mutual. Errol
never returned to the region where he spent twenty-five eventful
years, the first half of his short but exotic life. His only forays
in that direction were occasional jaunts to Hawaii, although in
the 1950s he made a movie in India and also visited Japan and
South Korea. Had he wished to do so, a side-trip Down Under
to see old cronies, friends, and relatives—even "Madge Parks"
perhaps—would not have been out of the question. For one
who traveled so constantly it is somewhat odd that Flynn kept
Australia, Tasmania, and New Guinea at arm's length. One
can only conclude that either he did not want to see that area
again or harbored some deep-seated misgivings concerning
what he had done there.

On 4 May, 1968, the *Sunday Examiner-Express* of
Launceston, Tasmania, the island's second largest city, printed
a strange tale by Robert Barratt describing an interview with
Bob Bellamy, "a grizzled, tattooed Canadian who skippered
the *Zaaca* [*sic*] during the last year of Flynn's life". Entitled
"The Truth About Errol Flynn, it was anything but.

Bellamy, an elderly seaman temporarily laid up ashore in
a hospital bed in British Columbia, told Barratt he was very
distressed by the star's death. "They broke the mould that
Errol came in; they just don't make men like him any more."
He said he first met Flynn in New Guinea in 1936.

> I remember a moving picture outfit came to Port
> Moresby, and they wanted to use Errol's yacht to make
> a picture. He insisted on being skipper of his own yacht,

and when the picture was shown he turned out better than the star, and that's how he got his start.

This old salt claims he rendezvoused with Errol in Hollywood ten years later for a few drinks at a joint on Sunset Strip, and then the two old friends got together again in 1957. Flynn was now seriously ill, but he insisted Bellamy accompany him on one final fling about the Pacific on the *Zaaca*.

The first stop was Tahiti where their host was Leeteg, "the wild German painter". Not realizing how sick Errol really was, the drunken Leeteg often grappled with the ailing star in riotous horseplay. But, Bellamy notes, Flynn was not one to walk away from a punch-up.

> He was always a heck of a fighter. He used to have a habit of seeing how many police he could lick in one night. I remember he ended up in gaol one night after taking on half the Rabaul police force.

With Flynn taking huge doses of heroin to kill the pain in his decaying liver they sailed on to Tonga for more parties, including one given in their honor by Queen Salote Tubou. In Auckland Errol became so ill that he had to spend several days ashore under a doctor's care. Then the *Zaaca* cruised across the Tasman Sea to Sydney and anchored in Rushcutter's Bay on the south side of the harbor. Although still sick, Flynn made a nostalgic visit to the Domain, a well-known Sydney park.

> One night we went ashore, and he took me to this dark little cave near the Domain. He told me he slept on the stone bench in the cave when he first arrived in Sydney from Hobart.
>
> We just sat there drinking a bottle of rum and looking out over the bay, and Errol talked about the fun it had been in the early days when he didn't have a penny and lived like a tramp.

While in Sydney, Bellany says he told his old friend about a fortune in pearls supposedly hidden by a Chinaman on Palawan Island. Flynn, who, as we know, had a penchant for jewels, immediately became interested, so they upped anchor and set out for the Philippines. This on-the-spot decision, according to Bellamy, "almost certainly" shortened the star's life. "He was in pretty bad shape at the time and I don't think the climate was doing him much good, but we headed off anyway.

*En route* northward this unpredictable pair stopped at Port Moresby, which they found disappointing. All of their old haunts had disappeared. "The only place we recognized was the post office." Off Timor Flynn became so sick that Bellamy headed the *Zaaca* for Darwin.

> The pilot came out and took him, and that was the last I ever saw of him, no goodbyes or anything. As soon as I could get ashore, I grabbed a cab and went to the hospital, but they told me Errol had been taken to Sydney. I found out later he was flown to Los Angeles, and died afterwards in Vancouver.

Bellamy says his good friend was generous to a fault and treated all women with respect, even those who swam out and crawled aboard the *Zaaca*. Yet women rarely were mentioned during their meandering cruise around the blue Pacific. "Seems funny when you think of all that publicity, but he seldom spoke about women. They just didn't seem to bother him much at all."

Shortly before they parted in Darwin, Errol, racked by constant pain, remarked to his skipper-friend: "You know, Bob, there is only one thing that I am scared of, and that is that after I die someone will find $10 in my pocket that I forgot to spend."

Gripping stuff, what? After trying to unravel Flynn's fictions about himself it seems pointless to dissect monstrous untruths concocted by alleged associates. But, just a few random comments. The *Zaca*, not the "Zaaca", was moored in Majorca during these years and certainly made no trip to the South Seas, nor does Flynn's itinerary (1957-9) appear to include any such jaunt. One basic consideration: Errol simply could not afford such a luxury. Instead, he was busy with movies, television appearances, even an ill-fated fling in legitimate theater . . . anything to make a few bucks and bolster his sagging career.

Skipper Bellamy could not have met Flynn in Port Moresby in 1936 (he left there three years earlier), and the elusive movie-making venture he describes so vividly presumably took place on the north coast of New Guinea circa 1929-30, not in the Moresby area . . . and there's some doubt as to whether it occurred at all! Yet, like Flynn's own stories, Bob Bellamy's yarns probably contain a bit of truth here and there. A picture in the *Sunday Examiner-Express* shows him displaying clippings and photos detailing his life with the Hollywood star to a somewhat bored nurse. The grizzled Canadian perhaps knew Flynn and may even have worked aboard the *Zaca* sometime in the 1950s, but this rambling South Sea travelogue seems to be based more upon the printed word than on fact.

Bellamy has picked random snatches from *My Wicked, Wicked Ways* and an episode or two from *Rascals in Paradise* (New York, 1957) by James Michener and A. Grove Day, or perhaps he read issues of *Hawaiian Life* used by these authors when they compiled Chapter 10, "Leeteg, the Legend". These fragments have been pieced together in a most alarming fashion. Edgar William Leeteg, born in East St. Louis, Illinois, on 13 April, 1904, did live in Tahiti in the 1930s and 1940s and gained considerable renown for his velvet paintings. However, he died in 1953 at least five years prior to the cruise this imaginative skipper says took place during the last year of Flynn's life. God knows, Errol Leslie Thomson Flynn could create enough fiction about himself and do it in a smooth, polished, urbane manner. He needed no help from rank amateurs of this sort.

# *Chapter Seven*

## Postscript: Reflections Upon Phallic Immortality

Thanks to divorces, a tumultuous rape trial, and various exploits on and off the screen, the last half of Errol Flynn's life (1934-59) is more-or-less an open book. Box office successes such as *Captain Blood, The Charge of the Light Brigade, The Adventures of Robin Hood,* and *Dawn Patrol* made him public property, as well as one of the most valuable performers in the Warner Brothers stable. His pencil-thin moustache, devil-may-care charm, lilting smile, roguish arrogance, and superb body were admired by millions.

For a decade (1936-46) Flynn was one of a half dozen stars (Clark Gable, Tyrone Power, etc.) who represented the epitome of male beauty. The celebrated courtroom confrontation of 1943 and failure to don a uniform during World War II made little, if any, dent in this international image. American GIs who followed those sensational proceedings merely thought Errol Flynn damned lucky—lucky to have gotten laid, lucky to have beaten the rap, and lucky to be a civilian! Very few individuals knew that the star, despite his elan and derring-do, was not in top physical condition. Writing in *Quadrant* (Spring, 1961), an Australian journal, Eric Feldt heaped scorn upon his fellow countryman, not realizing firstly that he had become a naturalized citizen of the United States in August of 1942 and, secondly, suffered from a weak heart.

> It would not occur to many to enquire what this bold hero did when war broke out, giving him a chance to show his real mettle. Gable and Stewart served with distinction but the swashbuckling Flynn stayed in

Hollywood, making money, drinking and fornicating, an Australian in the United States, safe from conscription.

In this role of cinema celebrity complete with unrestrained flamboyance, excessive adulation, and an income of some $200,000 per year, the boy from Hobart discovered joy as well as sadness and frustration. It was wonderfully exhilarating for both actor and audience as long as he could make those graceful leaps from castle walls and thrust home the slender sword. But by 1950 he was forty, approaching middle age, somewhat less agile, and carrying the heavy burden of fifteen years of publicity and high living.

Not only was Errol Flynn changing, but so were movie fans themselves. The cool, plastic good looks of the thirties were no longer in fashion. Audiences now wanted realism up there on the big screen, not escapism nor the antics of picture-perfect people. Trying to cope with these diverse factors, personal as well as professional, in 1949 Flynn made *That Forsyte Woman* with Greer Garson for Metro-Goldwyn-Mayer, his first movie away from Warner Brothers and a startling departure from his dashing, blood-and-guts past.

Yet, try as he might, Errol found it extremely difficult to age gracefully both on and off the screen. Mrs. Charles Chauvel of Sydney hit the nail squarely on the head when she said Flynn was "a male butterfly". Like some brightly colored, graceful insect he had had his moment of brilliance, but summer was ending and there was a hint of frost in the air. Soames Forsyte was a far cry from *The Sea Hawk* and *They Died with Their Boots On*. Fans found it impossible to accept their hero in such sedate surroundings, so Errol turned to *Captain Fabian, The Master of Ballantrae*, and *Crossed Swords*. He succeeded only in appearing increasingly ridiculous and obviously ill at ease.

Away from the camera Flynn fought the aging process with more and more liquor, experimentation with drugs long before it was the "in" thing to do, constant travel, and younger and younger women. Four years before his death, while making a movie in England, a member of the cast said he was consuming at least one and sometimes two bottles of champagne "to get the juices flowing" each morning. Both Errol and Nora Eddington (Mrs. Flynn # 2), the young blonde whom he met at a cigar counter in the Los Angeles County Courthouse during the rape trial, wrote openly of his bout with narcotics. She was fifteen years his junior. Lili had been five years older than Errol, and Patrice Wymore (Mrs. Flynn # 3 and his widow) was twenty-four to Flynn's forty-one when they were married at a Lutheran Church in Nice in October of 1950.

Beverly Aadland, his last playmate, was, according to her devoted mother's *The Big Love*, conceived in an apartment on Hollywood's Mariposa Avenue on the night of 7 December, 1941. The Pearl Harbor baby and Errol began seeing each other in 1957 when little Bev, a dancer in *Marjorie Morningstar*, was fifteen. This early spring-autumn pair spent considerable time together during Errol's last two years, and Beverly—"S. C., my small companion" . . . "my Woodsie", short for wood nymph—was with him in Vancouver when he died in mid-October of 1959. Toasting his memory in "pink bubbly" as Flynn had asked her to do, Miss Aadland told reporters he lived with a premonition of death, yet she quickly added that they had planned to marry and live in Jamaica as soon as he was divorced from Patrice Wymore.

The following day Miss Aadland tried a repeat of the "pink bubbly" ritual in a Seattle bar but was tossed out for being under age. Immediately after the star's death it looked as if there might be a sordid struggle over his final resting place. Wymore said he would be buried in Hollywood; Aadland, Jamaica. As his legal spouse and heir, Patrice of course prevailed.

Some two years later, after several kicks in the teeth by both the law and cruel fate, Beverly, mama, and an unidentified friend made a bizarre dawn pilgrimage to the star's grave in Forest Lawn Cemetery. Reverting to her wood nymph role,

Bev led her companions in a gay frolic over the well manicured plots, gathering flowers as they went. These they heaped high around Flynn's headstone. Mrs. Aadland tells in *The Big Love* how her daughter knelt, kissed the wet grass, and then cried out in alarm that she had heard a big belly laugh come surging up from Forest Lawn's rich soil. Apparently this made everyone above ground feel much, much better, for a few moments later they drove out of the Garden of Everlasting Peace waving joyous farewells to dear, dear Errol.

Actually, Flynn's heftiest after-life laugh may have come when and if he read his obituary in the staid *New York Times*. It saluted Errol as the "perennial Hollywood glamour boy" and then launched into a life story resplendent with tidbits even the man himself forgot to include in *My Wicked, Wicked Ways*. According to the *Times*, he attended yet another school as a youth—Lycee Louis le Grand in Paris, began his working days as second cook on an ocean-going steamer, and served as a "member of the New Guinea Constabulary in Papua". Then, added the *Times*, the unpredictable young Tasmanian became a newspaper correspondent in Sydney "and here everyone thought he had finally settled down". It is not necessary to point out that even Errol Flynn's obituary was semi-true, semi-false.

But, to return to the live Flynn, belly laughs six feet up instead of six feet down. Despite drink, high living, a weak heart, attacks of malaria and gonorrhea, a liver disorder (God knows why!), and other physical problems, our boy held up amazingly well. By 1955, however, his gaiety was becoming a bit forced. At lunchtime he could stretch out in his dressing room with sandwiches and more champagne and tell Charles Chauvel (the Australian director of his first movie) that he hated to go out to restaurants. "Every goddamn waitress expects to have her ass pinched by me!" But as the day wore on and night fell, the Flynn of old reappeared once more.

Associates recall Errol often became frantic for companionship—especially if he had been drinking heavily or had to appear in public. The possibility that he might arrive at a party alone and womanless sometimes drove him to desperate measures. On one occasion following a television appearance he tried without success to enlist the company of script girls, telephone operators, usherettes—any unescorted female within arms length.

Other times luck was on his side. A few friends in Errol's Manhattan hotel suite watched one evening as their host, facing a small Stork Club shindig without a date, became more and more irritable and less and less interested in a night on the town. Then, manna from heaven, the telephone rang. It was a former Miss Sweden of several seasons back who happened to be in New York, and did Mr. Flynn remember meeting her? Can you join us at the Stork . . . only a small party of friends. "As soon as she said yes, clouds of gloom rolled away and the dashing Flynn of old was in the saddle once more. As their chat ended the star winked roguishly and issued this blunt warning to his companion-to-be: "And, honey, you'd better not wear any pants because your ass is gonna be on the grass before this evening is over!"

But the end was in sight and Errol knew it. Jaunty remarks and a sea of champagne could not keep him afloat much longer. *The Films of Errol Flynn* records the impressions of Nora Eddington and Director Arthur Hiller who both saw him a few weeks before his death. They remember a proud, but shattered old man tottering toward the grave, still strutting like a peacock as he went.

After 1955 nearly every newsman he encountered was offered the opportunity to ghostwrite his life story, although Flynn clearly intended to retain a lion's share of any profits. At length Earl Conrad, a well-known writer with numerous books to his credit, agreed to undertake the project. Late in 1958 he spent ten weeks with Flynn in Jamaica, and from their conversations came *My Wicked, Wicked Ways*. The book, which was supposed to appear in mid-October of 1959, the very week Errol succumbed to a sudden heart attack in British Columbia, ends with these words: "The second half-century looms up, but I don't feel the night is coming on". One cannot help but wonder if this final impudent sally may not have been added hurriedly to the final proof after the star's demise.

Conrad and Flynn put together a very frank, revealing book—too frank and too revealing to suit some folks mentioned in its pages. New Guinea residents were not the only individuals distressed by what they read, and subsequent British editions (although bearing the label "unabridged") were forty to fifty pages shorter than the original version. In addition to the New Britain/New Guinea massacre tale of the 1920s mentioned earlier, other deletions include stories about Errol's mother, Bruce Cabot, Maureen O'Hara, Lili Damita, Mike Curtiz, and the brothers Warner. In almost every instance the material left out reflects unfavorably upon individuals concerned. This is especially true of sequences involving Flynn's mother and his first wife, Lili Damita. He infers that mama had numerous extra-marital affairs, including a stint with the Aga Khan, and portrays the lovely Lili in a contemptible light. Except for boudoir gymnastics their union was, in his view, a disaster from beginning to end. He was forced to the altar, his bride turned out to have a very shallow mind, and (surprise) despite their sacktime rapture she was something of a lesbian to boot!

Two of Errol's many affairs are erased completely from British copies of the book. Perhaps overseas editors thought enough was enough. Anyway, thousands of non-American readers of *My Wicked, Wicked Ways* know nothing of Flynn's conquest of Amelia Holiphant (whoever in hell she was) and his two-continent romance with the Princess Irene, dynamic daughter of a Rumanian royal line, whom he referred to as "the Greek". Perhaps it is mere coincidence, but American editions of this book which found their way onto the shelves of Australian libraries have either disappeared or remain permanently "misplaced".

After their son's death, Professor and Mrs. Flynn talked of writing a sequel which would serve as an antidote, a corrective to some of the more flagrant lies. They were particularly disturbed by the word "wicked" in the title. An article appearing in Hobart's *Saturday Evening Express* (21 April, 1962) tells how "Theo" and Marelle, in their late seventies, were struggling in a small English seaside flat to produce this "labor or love", a book which would set aright the erroneous, world-wide impression of their boy. The professor said Errol definitely was *not* "a swashbuckling seducer, a soldier of fortune, a hell-raiser":

> He was a perfectly-mannered, soft-hearted gentleman, a considerate and dutiful son, and humorous company. He may have had weaknesses—but he was never *wicked*.

Errol's outstanding weakness, his father maintained, was an inordinate love of publicity, be it good or bad.

> His mother and I know he was very rough on himself in that book he wrote: *My Wicked, Wicked Ways*.

> He gave himself a rough deal. Most of the bad stories were made up and he left out lots of interesting but not scandalous features of his life.

> He only wrote it because he needed publicity badly at that time.

> Errol always told us never to deny anything the publicity people of his film company said about him—and many of the false stories about him started from that.

> But we feel it is not fair that the world should remember him as being like that when it is not true.

> Another of his weaknesses was that he was courteous to women, no matter what they were.

> His behaviour to women was always impeccable and it was used as a rod against him.

Women would never leave him alone. The way they pestered him was enough to make you lose all your faith in womanhood.

I know, I have stayed with him many times.

Women would swim out to his yacht naked—dreadful, embarrassing, and insolent.

If you are nice to women you are accused of all sorts of low motives.

He married well three times—but he was a rolling stone always looking for new people and new places. He could not make marriage work. . . .

One part of his life that has never been told is his Jamaica years.

He spent a lot of time at his estates there and took a great interest in the local life.

I was ill a few years before his death and he was a wonderful son to me then—he phoned all the time from wherever he was, and was wonderful to his mother during the difficult period.

I have never been at all disappointed in him.

He used his talents in leading the kind of life most men would like to lead but don't have the guts to.

The fact that he left us so much money shows he wasn't the playboy everyone thought he was. We are building a house in Sussex with the money he left us.

We hope that our book will lead more people to understand what a brave, well-mannered, and intelligent person Errol was.

Of course, this is a proud but troubled father speaking; and, like *My Wicked, Wicked Ways*, his words are a melange of truth and semi-truth distorted, one assumes, through aging paternal eyes. This son *was* many of the things the professor says he was and some of the things he vows he was not. Errol was kind to his parents after he became a star; but, as subsequent news stories have revealed, he was heavily in debt at the time of his death, largely as the result of a disastrous film venture in Italy in 1953, the never completed *William Tell*. As for this reply to a son's flamboyant autobiography, it never appeared. Lily Mary (Marelle) died in 1967 and "Theo" a year later.

The professor's life was in startling contrast to that of his son. T. T. once remarked to a reporter,

> There was never any chance of Errol following in my footsteps in an academic career—school to him was a place to let off high spirits, not a place where knowledge could be gained.

The elder Flynn's scientific research won him many honors. He was a fellow of the Linnaean Society, the International Institute of Embryology (Utrecht), and the Zoological Society, a member of the Royal Irish Academy, and in 1930-1 held a Rockefeller grant for research on the development of the monotreme ovum. His work as chief casualty officer in the civil defense forces of Belfast during World War II earned him an O.B.E. Professor Flynn's thirty-one line entry in the British *Who's Who* (1964), a compendium which studiously ignored his famous son, is studded with achievements.

There is no evidence that Mrs. Flynn bore any lasting ill-will toward Errol for what he wrote about her. In fact, the reverse is true. A letter to a relative written several years after his death notes that it is the birthday of "my darling boy". One suspects that since he obviously inherited much of his flair and dash from the Youngs, mama even may have reveled secretly in some of the publicity and attention which came her way as a result of his exploits. It is true Errol says his mother once told a Manhattan reporter that he was "a nasty little boy"—a statement deleted from some editions of the autobiography.

Despite the intimate detail found in *My Wicked, Wicked Ways*, the book raises more questions than it answers. Brushing aside the exaggerated stories, haphazard chronology, and screwed-up geography, where are the people who really helped

Errol Flynn during these formative, pre-Hollywood years? Where is Grandma Flynn with whom he lived from time to time in Sydney? Where is Ken Hunter-Kerr who introduced him to a select stratum of that city's society and got him a job when he got kicked out of the classroom for the last time? Where is Charles Chauvel, the man who gave him his first break in the movies? Why is the lady who bought him a yacht not given proper recognition. And, if Flynn actually thought Vera Giblin had done more for him than "anybody else on this earth", how come she plays such a minor role in this story? She was apparently the first individual to point him toward a theatrical career and provided (unintentionally it is true) a portion of the funds which started him on his way to stardom. These people—grandmother, mentor, employer, mother, protector-patroness—are key individuals in Flynn's early life, but he either ignores or denigrates them.

Why? There are at least two explanations, perhaps more. First, he seems determined not to share credit for his teenage development and rise to international fame with anyone. One grandmother is ridiculed; the other ignored. Lily Mary is portrayed in a sinister light, and the two men who did the most for him during his Sydney years (Hunter-Kerr and Chauvel) are forgotten. Also, some of the people who helped him on his way after 1934—Director Mike Curtiz, Lili Damita, the Warner brothers—are treated rather shabbily as their protests to his publishers reveal. Vera Giblin does receive scant, casual mention; and, to his credit, Flynn corresponded with this well-meaning benefactor long after he left New Guinea.

There is a second possibility. By the last months of 1958 when Flynn began to work on his autobiography he was a sick man. Perhaps drugs, liquor, and high living had exacted such a toll that truth and fiction became hopelessly blurred, although as we've seen Errol always had a remarkable propensity for the tall tale and was not one to leave stark reality unadorned. Some of his relatives believe ill health to be the more plausible explanation. They simply cannot conceive that, if mentally and physically alert, Flynn would have written some of the passages found in *My Wicked, Wicked Ways*.

But, since those stories form an integral part of the book it is intriguing to consider for a moment where Errol may have gotten them. What follows is, of course, pure conjecture. Flynn certainly picked up many of the tales he incorporated into his "life" in the bars of Rabaul, Salamaua, Wau, Sydney, Rockhampton, Cairns, and other communities he visited from time to time, yet specific individuals with whom he associated appear to have provided large segments of the early chapters of *My Wicked, Wicked Ways*.

From Forsythe, the man he met on Hinchinbrook Island in 1930, came the episode about illegal traffic in bird of paradise plumes in Dutch New Guinea. Charlie Burt, one suspects, told Errol of his days in the outback as they cruised along the Australian coast on the *Sirocco*, although it is still easy enough to hear stories about the vast continental hinterland from scores of suburbanites who have never seen it. Trelawney Adams, who became a schooner captain in the islands, may have provided another aspect of Flynn's pre-Hollywood career. However, the prime source of much of his New Guinea derring-do is the flamboyant Jack Hides. As a patrol officer, "Jack-a-Hides" lived many of the experiences his drinking buddy usurped as his own.

A Hollywood column appearing in the Melbourne *Argus* (12 September, 1936) saluted Flynn as a "peace-loving" man until he got into the movies, but then regaled eager readers with tales of exotic travel, gold strikes, experiences in pearl fishing and copra trading, and work as a short-story writer, schooner captain, and actor . . . hardly the stuff the average "peace-loving" career is made of. To this reporter Errol conceded he had actually been scared only once.

I was ambushed in New Guinea by a tribe of natives with a peeve, or something. They sprang from the jungle, bows and arrows ready. My boys dropped their loads and ran. . . . My gunbearer—he's usually the last one to stick—dropped my gun and left for parts unknown.

Grabbing my trusty pistol, I winged one of my attackers on my way out. My only scar is on my shin, and was put there by a poisoned arrow that struck me as I made tracks away from there.

I kept on going until I came to a clearing. Pouring rain added to the jolly occasion. There I stayed all night, twisting my head to watch in all directions. The worst of it was that, although I had cigarettes, I had no matches. Miserable night! A smoke and no way to light it!

Next morning my boys came back, sheepishly, finding me drenched and very, very irritable. They back-tracked and got the load—including the matches—and I smoked instantly.

This report concludes with an unlikely flourish concerning Lili Damita's engagement ring and (once more) those diamonds. Errol claims that while in New Guinea he picked up a stone which he wrapped in rags and stuffed into his pocket "never dreaming that it would be a symbol of my love for one of the most sophisticated and beautiful women of the world". This last bit about long-cherished jewels is obviously false (no one else has ever found diamonds in New Guinea), but the altercation with wild natives sounds very much like something which might have happened to Jack Hides.

Then there's the mystery of Joel Swartz/Dr. Gerrit H. Koets/Dr. Herman F. Erben. From all indications they are one and the same person, although Swartz (we are told) is American, Koets, German, and Erben, Austro-American. Perhaps it is easiest to deal with each in order of appearance. Swartz, a key figure in the novel *Showdown*, was a moviemaker who hired Shamus O'Thames's schooner, the *Maski*, to photograph head-hunters up the Sepik River. In 1932, according to *My Wicked, Wicked Ways*, Swartz cabled Flylnn to come to Tahiti to play the role of Fletcher Christian in a movie based upon the *Bounty* legend. This same book discloses that the Sepik trip (now featuring Errol Flynn and not Shamus O'Thames) actually was a super-sleuth job for the American and British governments which were photographing the northern New Guinea coast in anticipation of war with Japan.

Dr. Gerrit H. Koets, who bears a remarkable resemblance to the real-life Erben, entered Flynn's life at Rabaul as he was leaving the islands for London in 1933. Koets, a huge man, had been doing medical research in northern Australia and was loaded down with cameras and other paraphernalia. The two men became stalwart buddies as they whorehoused their way for some eight months through China, South Asia, India, Africa, and France. They parted in Marseilles, and Errol heaped praise upon this "wonderful friendship between men".

> This man was the great influence in my life. He showed me in a humorous, bawdy, Rabelaisian, tough, rough way the difference between a man with a soul and a man without one, even though neither of us was sure what a soul was.

Early in 1937, according to the autobiography, the two men resumed their global romp in a tour which took them from Hollywood to Chicago to Paris to Madrid . . . although their true goal was Brazil! A film capital report published in the *New York Times* (28 February, 1937) said Errol was off to the Amazon jungles to search for Paul Redfern, a long lost American flyer. Circumstances surrounding this venture and the circuitous approach to the continent of South America are indeed perplexing. (Errol writes in *My Wicked, Wicked Ways* that a recurrence of gonorrhea made an extended overseas visit most attractive to him personally.)

The ebullient young actor had just published *Beam Ends* (which this Hollywood spokesman dubbed "a goofy Odyssey"), was working on a script in which he planned to star, "White Rajah", based upon the life of Sir James Brooke of Sarawak, and now was setting off for South America by way of Europe. This reporter credited Errol's "picturesque and sometimes incredible friend, Dr. Herman F. Erben, the anthropologist", with stirring Flynn's interest in Redfern. However, before heading south the unpredictable pair were going 6,000 miles due east to visit Professor and Mrs. Flynn in Northern Ireland and then on to Madrid where Errol would view the war as a roving reporter for an English press syndicate.

Thus Flynn's companion in Spain was not Koets, but Erben—at least that is the name cited in dispatches from Madrid in April of 1937. On the 5th Erben, who said he was from New York, told reporters his actor friend was "slightly wounded over the left eye by a rebel machine gun bullet in the University City area". However, a simultaneous United Press cable from Valencia stated that Flynn had been seen at a nearby beach and was "in the best of health", although he eluded newsmen trying to question him. The following day officials of the Republican government denied Erben's story.

If nothing else, this episode sheds some light upon the good doctor. Press coverage indicates he served in the Austrian army during World War I and was a specialist in both tropical diseases and exotic adventure. He had led expeditions to the far corners of the globe and twice had the pleasure of denying official reports of his own death. Herman F. sure sounds like a fine foil for E. Flynn. What happened to Paul Redfern and the trip to South America is anyone guess.

Twelve years later Errol told a New York reporter how he met Dr. Herman F. Erban [*sic*] at Rabaul about 1930, and then proceeded to describe their photographic jaunt up the Sepik River aboard his ketch, the *Sirocco*. So, round and round she does! Swartz, Koets, Erben, Swartz and Koets appear to be fictitious; Erben, real. Yet, it is remarkable that in his potpourri of recollections Errol can hail in florid tones "the great influence in my life" but cite an incorrect name for the individual so honored.

Errol's sister, Rosemary, recalls meeting Dr. Erben in the 1930s. She thought him "a rather bogus, free-wheeling scientist of doubtful reputation who had endeared himself greatly to Errol". Twenty years later, while she and her husband were in West Germany, at Errol's request they tried to locate Erben, but discovered he had disappeared behind the Iron Curtain.

In addition to telling us something about the elusive Erben, the Madrid affair evoked instant response from Hollywood. Douglas W. Churchill, writing in the *New York Times* (18 April, 1937), said Warner Brothers was very "vexed" over what had occurred.

> Mr. Flynn is a sort of super-Richard Halliburton of the movies. His adventurous life and daring exploits have long served the fan magazines with amazing yarns. Jungles, steppe [?], and bush have known this intrepid actor, and the fan magazines, encouraged by the studio, have made the most of it. The faith of some of the brethren was shaken during the filming of 'Another Dawn' when Mr. Flynn experienced some difficulty in remaining astride a horse, an incident not in harmony with stories of his adventures on the great cattle ranches of Australia.

According to Churchill, Warner's was thinking of sending a staff publicity spokesman with their star whenever he ventured far afield in the future.

When *My Wicked, Wicked Ways* appeared, some who knew Flynn in the Southwest Pacific scorned the work as a fake, a damned pack of lies from cover to cover. The *Pacific Islands Monthly* denounced the New Guinea sequences as "largely piffle". Others who were associated with this young man in Sydney, Rabaul, and Port Moresby were flabbergasted by how much he actually did reveal. Over and over they have shaken their heads in disbelief as they talked about Flynn, "By God, it's all there! Exaggerated, of course, but that's just old Flynny and his ways." While events may not have unfolded precisely as described and may not have involved Errol himself, there is almost always some element of truth, some kernel of reality hidden deep in each episode. Anyone who read *Beam Ends* with its small dash of literary license in the final chapters should have been prepared for the full-blown, bigger-than-life canvas painted in the autobiography.

Flynn's three books are a mix of personal experience, fiction, and contemporary events stirred together by a master raconteur. They are, if you wish, highly flavoured "composite" history. Using his own life as a skeletal framework he adds to it numerous amusing, entertaining tales. This is something many of us do in day-to-day conversation. We make ourselves more interesting, more appealing by lying just a little bit. Bland, routine incidents often become transformed into enjoyable, worth-telling anecdotes. A novelist or short-story writer may collect these fragments and weave them into a single fabric and be hailed as a genius. Errol Flynn does much the same thing; and, because he has the audacity to label the product "autobiography" and live in a bizarre fashion his work is "piffle".

This is no attempt to elevate E. L. T. Flynn to the ranks of literary immortals. He was an entertaining, highly readable writer, possessing therein at least two attributes frequently not found in many published works. Errol probably could have made a living as a journalist or short-story writer. With his flair and charm he might also have been a success as a public relations man or a theatrical entrepreneur. He had the connections in the Sydney business community circa 1926-33 which could have boosted him on his way.

He certainly had brains . . . no doubt about it. But he possessed a fatal flaw. And, despite his father's candid assertions, it was not his inordinate love of publicity. Errol was, to put it bluntly, goddamned lazy. Why spend time and effort learning a trade or a profession when through wit, physical charm, guile, and theft one could shortcut his way to wealth and ease? This attitude, which some might term eminently practical, is especially apparent in his career before the camera. While his golden age in Hollywood (1935-42) produced some wondrous swashbuckling, Errol Flynn was not really acting at all or even exerting himself to any unusual degree. He was merely transferring a natural style developed in Sydney, Port Moresby, Rabaul, and London to a much larger audience. Individuals who knew him at Hobart High, Shore, or in the islands underscore this truth.

Errol Flynn, the actor, only came to grips with his profession when those native instincts which won him quick fame and easy fortune began to fail. In his last years, no longer able to rely upon rapier thrusts and slim elegant profile, he had to learn his craft and really work at acting as never before. Youth was gone, and the formula movie of the 1930s had also vanished. This did wring out of Flynn one of his best performances as the worldly Mike Campbell in *The Sun Also Rises*, although cynical detractors would maintain that he was merely being his natural, now dissipated self.

What remained (after 1943 especially) was a nightmarish reputation as a roguish Romeo, a phallic performer of remarkable genius and consummate inventiveness. Australian schoolgirls, nurtured on the late, late show and lavatory gossip, contrived to spread the rumor that one of their nation's best-known exports was possessed of unsurpassed endowment. Some, it is said, were much distressed by the dedication found in *My Wicked, Wicked Ways*: "To a Small Companion". Only the revelation that this referred to Beverly Aadland, Flynn's final female, restored Errol to his proper place in their adoring eyes.

Simply put, the tragedy of Errol Flynn is that he became a prisoner of his public image. This truth is brought home very forcefully in the final pages of *The Films of Errol Flynn* by several individuals closely associated with him during the last decade of his life. Hollywood, the publicity staff at Warner

Brothers, and millions of fans who wallowed vicariously in the alleged sexual exploits of this beautiful man created a monster which eventually triumphed over reality.

Flynn's love-hate relationship with his public image (the emphasis definitely being on *love* much of the time) was complicated by other factors. Despite his erotic reputation and a constant craving for female companionship, Errol Flynn really didn't like women. Young Ben Parer sensed this fact while drinking with him at Mrs. Stewart's pub in the New Guinea highlands in 1933. His tempestuous on-and-off marriages support this assertion, and Flynn himself on occasions agreed. In a snippet cut from later editions of *My Wicked, Wicked Ways* he remarked while discussing the demise of his life with Lily Damita:

> I sometimes think that in one way Lili and I were somewhat alike. It is possible that she essentially disliked men and that I essentially disliked women.

This comment, also found in the autobiography, highlights yet another dilemma.

> I know there are two men inside of me. One wants to ramble and has rambled around the globe more than once, in the sky and below the water. The other man is a settled fellow, who thinks sometimes he is or ought to be a husband-man, and that he should sit settled in a house by the side of the road or by the side of the sea.

This dual, contradictory yearning is, of course, by no means unique to Errol Flynn. Millions of men in all ages, while drawn to the attractions of hearth and family, have wrestled with the urge to roam free and far. Considering Flynn's footloose career, one might at first reject this statement as simply more public relations fluff or another of our hero's semi-truthful dreams given verbal form; however, there is evidence to support this assertion. Writing in 1969 of his years in the United States army, Elliott R. Thorpe recorded his impressions of Flynn in the late 1930s. Thorpe was then stationed in the Hawaiian

Islands. He met the famous screen personality at a modest country club on the island of Maui and found him to be "an intelligent conversationalist".

> During his first week on the island he was a pleasant, courteous, unassuming chap who seemed to enjoy the view of Haleakala from the club porch. All agreed the stories about Flynn must be exaggerations. He suddenly flew back to Honolulu and quickly returned with a feminine companion who could not have been described as being a 'homebody'. Then the good-looking Aussie came to life and gave the island something to talk about. At the end of the second week, it was decided the actor's ebullient spirits would be more appreciated in Honolulu, and he was seen safely aboard a Honolulu-bound craft. His visit enlivened local conversation for quite a while.

In his last days Errol clearly recognized the true nature of his tragedy. He regretted deeply (at times) the phallic Flynn and talked (also at times) of how he should have been a writer, not a movie actor. Actually his writing record is more than adequate, one which any semi-professional might envy. All of his books were published simultaneously in New York and London. Both *My Wicked, Wicked Ways* and *Showdown* joined the paperback ranks, and the latter was published independently in Sydney (Invincible Press) and in Stockholm (Wahlström & Windstrand). In addition, that novel had the signal honor of being banned—in of all places—Ireland, although with typical Gaelic dispatch it took the Irish six years to reach that decision.

In October of 1959, commenting upon the death of its most famous son, the *Hobart Mercury* reported Flynn had told newsmen in Vancouver that he was no longer interested in films. "The rest of my life will be devoted to women and litigation". This flippant remark casts a strange light upon this man's complex dilemma. He saw clearly his chief faults and recognized those factors which both created and smashed his life; yet, facing reporters for perhaps the last time, he could not resist the temptation to say something—true or false—which would make good, readable copy.

Errol was, from all indications, a reporter's delight. Always charming, witty to the end. An Australian newsman who met many of the Hollywood great in the 1950s and detailed their comings and goings for thousands of Down Under readers remembers the star greeting him erect and elegant with glass in hand and boasting in confident tones: "Before you stands the only man ever to cross the Atlantic four times in a dressing gown!" He says only one other screen luminary (Gary Cooper) surpassed Flynn in his gracious, considerate attitude toward the working press.

But those few words, that brief sentence about women and litigation tossed out in a crowded airport waiting room, can hardly stand as an epitaph for a man like Errol Flynn. Instead, let's look back to some of those lines found in his New Guinea notebook.

I am going to front the essentials of life to see if I can learn what it has to teach and above all not to discover when I come to die, that I have not lived.

We fritter our lives away in detail, but I am not going to do this. I am going to live deeply, to acknowledge not one of the so-called social forces which hold our lives in thrall & reduce us to economic dependency. The best part of life is spent earning money in order to enjoy a questionable liberty during the least valuable part of it.

I am going . . . to drive life into a corner & reduce it to its lowest terms and if I find it mean than I'll know its meanness, and if I find it sublime I shall know it by experience—and not make wistful conjectures about it conjured up by illustrated magazines.

To learn what is worth one's while is the largest part of the Art of Life. . . . The value, the intrinsic value, of our actions, emotions, thoughts, possessions, way of life, occupations, of the manner in which we are living—this is the first thing to be determined; for, unless we are *satisfied* that any of these things have a true value, even if only relative, our lives are futile, and there is no more hopeless realization than this.

Errol Flynn most certainly "fronted up" to life, spent money as fast as he earned it (and then some), and learned about life from first-hand experience. Sadly, only when it was much too late did he realize that he had forgotten to follow his own dictates. He had failed to discern the basic first principles of what in the hills of New Guinea he once termed the "Art of Life". Recognition of this colossal blunder, perhaps as much as any physical ill, caused him to wither and die.

Writer, adventurer, con man, screen star, Don Juan to a distraught and disturbed generation, frustrated in marriage and career, butt of sexual jokes and sly smirks ("in like Flynn"), bouts with disease, drink, and drugs, and then sudden death at the age of fifty. Surely there is great tragedy in this life, but one can hear the chorus of would-be satyrs as they sing their sceptical paean amid glasses of beer and hazy fantasies of carnal delight: "What a tragedy . . . what a way to go!" Errol, debonair and smiling, belly laugh, roguish wink and all, probably would agree.

# Chapter Eight

## Postscript # 2 – A Legend Under Fire

Since 1975, thanks to late-night television, the ever-present appeal of swashbuckling tales, and several provocative studies of his life and times, Errol L. T. Flynn lives on as lustily as ever. These publications include, in chronological order, Lionel Godfrey, *The Life and Crimes of Errol Flynn* (New York: St. Martin's Press & London: Robert Hale, Ltd., 1977); Earl Conrad, *Errol Flynn: A Memoir* (New York: Dodd, Mead & Co., 1978); Michael Freedland, *The Two Lives of Errol Flynn* (London: Arthur Barker, Ltd., 1978), issued by William Morrow of New York in 1979; Charles Higham, *Errol Flynn: The Untold Story* (Garden City: Doubleday & Co., 1980); Peter Valenti, *Errol Flynn: A Bio-Biography* (Westport, Conn. & London: Greenwood Press, 1984); Buster Wiles, with William Donati, *My Days with Errol Flynn* (Santa Monica: Roundtable Publishing, 1988), Tony Thomas, *Errol Flynn: The Spy Who Never Was* (New York: Citadel Press, 1990); and Lawrence Bassoff, *Errol Flynn: The Movie Posters* (Beverly Hills: Lawrence Bassoff Collection, 1995).

Several of these books eventually made their way into paperback ranks, although it should be noted, when Higham told his "untold story" in 1980 *My Wicked, Wicked Ways* was in its fourteenth printing. Meanwhile, British author Gerry Connelly of 65 Constable Road, Corby, Northamptonshire (NN 18 ORT), has produced two very complete accounts of our hero's stage career—*Errol Flynn in Northampton*. The first edition appeared in 1994, the second in 1998. Connelly explores in depth a period in Errol's life often ignored by others. He establishes Errol participated in the Malvern Festival in the summer of 1934 and subsequently appeared briefly in Glasgow and London before gaining minor film roles that would take him to Hollywood.

In 1996 Hart Ryan Productions of London unveiled a well-received, hour-long documentary on Flynn, part of the "Secret Lives" series aired on Channel 4, and two years later E-Entertainment produced an American version. Then in 2007 Flaming Star Films of East Melbourne, Australia, released a third TV documentary entitled "Tasmanian Devil: The Fast and Furious Life of Errol Flynn." And Flynn fans may wish to consult this fine web site—"Jack Marino's Salute to the Fabulous Flynn." Available online at <http://www.warrior-filmmakers.com/errolflynn/index.html>. Last accessed on 14 July 2008.

Perhaps Errol's most avid fan of recent decades is Eric George Lilley, president and founder of the International Errol Flynn Society—address "Hollywood," 2 Holly Close, Crookham Park, Crookham Common, Newbury, Berkshire, England (RG 19 8 QZ).

Although some authors and film directors accept too readily the word of *My Wicked, Wicked Ways*, several of these books possess distinct merit. Godfrey's "Life and Crimes," although brief, has a fine bibliography, excellent photos, a unique guide to recordings of musical scores from Flynn films, and something often missing from such works, an index! Conrad's "Memoir" is a valiant attempt by the talented writer who "ghosted" *My Wicked, Wicked Ways* to describe the male phenomenon that was literally fading into oblivion during the struggle to complete that autobiography. Conrad, by the way, enjoyed the full cooperation of the Flynn family while composing his "Memoir."

The opening chapters of Freedland's book are little more than a re-write of lines found in *My Wicked, Wicked Ways*. However, once Flynn gets to Hollywood and becomes a star, his interviews paint a more complete picture. Nevertheless, the reader, forced to sit through what seems to be the world's longest picture show (one Flynn epic after another), is left wondering what *two* lives our hero led. That number, some may conclude, is both restrictive and misleading.

Higham, on the other hand, provides lives aplenty. His Errol, in addition to being a screen idol and consummate womanizer, is a Nazi spy and bisexual lover of Tyrone Power, Howard Hughes, Truman Capote, and Appolinio Diaz (an Acapulco beach boy), as well as an international criminal and smuggler of gold, guns, and drugs. His "untold story" includes a brief list of books, films, and plays relating to Flynn and a ten-page inventory of DECLASSIFIED SECRET DOCUMENTS that presumably shed light upon the mysterious Dr. Erben and link his exploits to those of Errol.

Valenti's "Bio-Biography" is a quite different venture. A scholarly work indeed, it presents the reader with a succinct, one-hundred-page biography, followed by seventy pages of "filmography," a list of radio and TV appearances, and nearly forty pages of bibliographic sources, letters, and interviews. Valenti, a professor of English at Fayetteville State University in North Carolina, also provides a terse but penetrating analysis of Higham's Nazi ties.

No specific charges of espionage ever were lodged against Flynn, he writes, and no documentary evidence to support such charges exists. The film star, according to Valenti, was being defamed for association with unsavory individuals who may never have had anything to do with espionage. And, whenever Flynn's name surfaces, those making the charges usually are characterized by other observers as "unstable." Valenti concedes Flynn's trip to Spain in 1937 caused concern in some quarters, as did his friendship with playboys such as Freddy McEvoy and Carlos Verjarano y Cassina, as well as his on-and-off relationship with the eccentric and flamboyant Dr. Erben. But, he concludes, hard evidence to support Higham's sensational claims simply does not exist.

In still stronger terms, Buster Wiles, William Donati, and Tony Thomas make much the same argument. Donati helped Wiles—a stunt man who worked with Flynn and became a close friend—describe "his days" with the screen star, and he adds to this rollicking narrative a devastating, fifty-page appendix on "The Flynn Controversy." He takes Higham to task for providing no footnotes and no explanation of once-secret documents that allegedly connect Flynn to wartime espionage.

Donati agrees Errol was investigated by the U. S. government from time to time, primarily because of his Spanish fling and the fact that he consorted with questionable characters. In his quest for the truth, Donati traveled to Vienna in September 1980 and interviewed at length the elusive Dr. Hermann F. Erben, then eighty-three years of age. Erben, who died in January 1985, conceded he was investigated by U. S. authorities, but the trouble arose, he said, from an incident in 1938 involving drugs, not espionage. At that time he was a ship's doctor and American customs officials suspected he was dealing in illegal substances. Whatever the truth, it is patently clear Erben (for some years a naturalized U. S. citizen) displayed a rather casual attitude toward rules and regulations relating to international travel. As for rumors of bisexuality, both friend Wiles and medical man Erben dismiss such talk as utterly ridiculous.

Tony Thomas, veteran teller of silver-screen tales and author of some thirty books, tackles the "untold story" head-on and emerges triumphant. The result is a sensitive, carefully researched portrait dedicated, by the way, to Earl Conrad. Thomas knew Flynn during the last four years of his life and worked closely with him while making recordings for the Canadian Broadcasting Company. In ten chapters he takes aim at numerous Higham charges and usually scores a direct hit.

The supreme irony of this 186-page rebuttal is disclosure by Thomas that Flynn, to use his word, "dabbled" in British intelligence during an extensive tour of South America in the summer of 1940 (work that elicited personal praise from President Roosevelt) and subsequently offered to spy, not for Adolph Hitler, but for the Allied cause. In February 1942—having been rejected for military service because of health problems—Flynn broached the subject in a lengthy letter to William J. Donovan, soon to become head of the Office of Strategic Services (OSS). His father, he explained, was well-known in all parts of Ireland, he himself was an easily recognized personality thanks to his film career, and, if clothed in an American uniform, he might be able to keep a wary eye on German agents operating in the Irish republic. Few, he noted, would expect a movie star to be meddling in such matters.

Nothing came of this offer, but seven months later Flynn landed a job as war correspondent for Hearst papers. However, joy quickly vanished when he was overwhelmed by sensational rape charges. Higham's "untold story" devotes some forty pages to the ensuing Betty Hansen-Peggy Satterlee saga, but apparently is silent concerning any offer to become an Allied agent. (The original 1980 edition lacks both table of contents and index.)

The Bassoff book—a truly handsome number produced in full color on pages 11" by 14"—contains a foreward by Stewart Granger, a glossary of movie-poster terminology, and a brief biography. It is a fine companion to *The Films of Errol Flynn* compiled by Tony Thomas, Rudy Behlmer, and Clifford McCarty and issued by Citadel Press in 1969.

To return to those pesky FBI files for a moment, some four hundred pages allegedly relating to Flynn now are available on the Internet. Although most names and entire paragraphs often are blacked out and the Bureau concedes the material sometimes does not actually pertain to Flynn, what remains discloses, above all else, overweening fascination with his sex life. . .did he violate the white slave act by taking nineteen-year-old Nora Eddington to Mexico. . .did employees of Warner Brothers routinely procure young girls for him??? But strangely, instead of ties to Nazi Germany, these pages hint at sympathy for the Communist cause; however, no reliable sources for such rumors are cited and Errol is only one of numerous stars fingered in a casual manner.

In the spring of 1940, at the request of J. Edgar Hoover, the Los Angeles bureau chief explored the possibility of recruiting Flynn and other luminaries to participate in patriotic, moral-boosting programs. Two years later, when gossip columnist Igor Cassini scoffed at Errol's Selective Service classification of 4-F, Hoover's interest was aroused once more. Intrigued, he shipped westward a clipping of Cassini's "These Charming People" (*Washington Times-Herald*), 19 June 1942) and asked local agents to investigate the matter "in a very discreet manner." Flynn's draft board duly reported he had been disqualified for military service by reason of "tuberculosis, pulmonary, chronic reinfection (adult), type in right apex."

These files disclose the ensuing rape trial spawned extortion threats to Flynn and allegations of still more lurid sexual exploits. They also include a rather detailed account of Dr. Erben's exotic life, which may or may not be true. Born and educated in Vienna, World War I veteran, tropical disease expert, world traveler, etc., Erben apparently first came to the United States in 1923 to continue his medical studies and soon filed papers leading to formal naturalization in 1930. During the decade that followed, he often worked as a ship's doctor, met Errol in New Guinea, and obtained a license to practice in several states, among them, Washington, Louisiana, New York, and New Jersey.

In 1938, presumably because of the drug problem mentioned earlier, he was forced to surrender his naturalization certificate and return to Europe. Yet two years later the good doctor was back in America where he gained an ever-so-brief appointment as surgeon at a Florida CCC camp. Much like Errol's short tenure as a New Guinea patrol officer, paper work soon caught up with Erben and he found himself facing court proceedings in San Francisco for failure, he says, to reside in America for a five-year period prior to naturalization.

While awaiting trial, Dr. Erben was recruited by the German secret service (Abwher) and agreed to join up, he insists, in order to *help* America. Anyway, this led to an assignment in China, arrest and imprisonment by the Japanese, release by American GIs, and then employment by the American government until his past entrapped him once more. In the late 1940s Erben was expelled to Germany. It's a wild tale, one worthy of the great Flynn himself.

During his South American tour—at the time Erben was facing possible deportation—Errol had an extensive conversation with the U. S. consular staff in Buenos Aires concerning his erratic friend and his problems. He praised Erben as a "magnificent physician" who seemed to become enmeshed in all sorts of "minor" difficulties and actually was something of a "screw-ball."

'But he was *not*, Errol insisted, an enemy agent. In fact, his movie star friend was of the opinion that Erben would not be very effective in that role since he often failed to carry proper papers and was so adept at breaking local rules and regulations. As a result, authorities usually were well aware of his whereabouts. Nevertheless, during these months Errol did contact the Los Angeles FBI office and Mrs. Eleanor Roosevelt in an effort to assist Dr. Erben as he faced court proceedings in San Francisco.

Hermann Friedrich Erben actually plays a small role in these files, although they disclose the Bureau expressed some concern over Flynn's contacts with Castro in the 1950s. All too often this material turns out to be a little more than random newspaper clippings and unsubstantiated rumor, rather dubious "documentation." What remains legible raises questions concerning the course of the FBI under Hoover's direction, and one cannot help but wonder why J. Edgar thought Errol Flynn's sex life endangered or even was related to our national well-being.

The story of what happened to the rest of our cast—much less colorful than the turbulent life of Dr. Erben—can be summed up rather quickly. Errol's parents, as noted earlier, died in the late 1960s. In 1947, sister Rosemary married Charles Warner, a career U. S. Air Force officer, who was posted from time to time in various parts of Europe and America. After living in Washington off and on, Colonel and Mrs. Warner retired to Limeuil, Dordogne, France in 1974. She died of cancer seven years later (age 61) in the Air Force Hospital in Landstuhl, Germany.

Following divorce in 1942, Errol's first wife, Lili Damita, married an Iowa businessman, Allen Loomis, and eventually retired to Florida, where she died in March 1994, age 92. Their son, Sean, born in May 1941, resembled his father physically and briefly pursued a screen career in Europe before becoming a news photographer. He disappeared in Cambodia in April 1970 while working as a CBS cameraman.

Errol and Nora Eddington had two daughters—Deirdre, born in January 1944, and Rory, March 1947. Deirdre has worked as a stunt girl, stand-in, and actress. Her sister, a model for a time, is married and has one son. Their mother, who divorced Flynn to marry singer Dick Haymes, later wed Richard Black, a Beverly Hills resident.

Third wife Patrice Wymore was the mother of a daughter, Arnella, born in Rome on Christmas Day 1953. Like half-sister Rory, Arnella tried her luck as a model, married, produced a son, and then was divorced. She died in Jamaica in 1998 following a bout with drugs. Beverly Aadland, Errol's young playmate at the time of his death, is married and living quietly in a small southern California community with her construction supervisor husband and teenage daughter, Aadlanda. Beverly and Nora's daughters reportedly hit it off rather well in the years after Errol died.

Patrice, now in her early eighties, apparently is holding forth in what remains of Errol's Jamaica estate, "Castle Comfort." The house, wrecked during a hurricane in 1988, has been the source, according to Sunday tabloids, of bitter family disputes, and Patrice (to the displeasure of Rory) is trying to sell the 2200-acre spread. Rory, along with other close relatives, long has been distressed by other twists in this ongoing saga—Errol's burial (at the insistence of widow Patrice) in Hollywood, not Jamaica, no headstone until Rory purchased one two decades after his death, rumors of multiple wills, alleged misuse of trust fund money, and so on.

If there's a common threat connecting those who knew Flynn, wrote about him, or merely admired his incomparable movie-screen elan from afar, it is a sense of bewilderment concerning what made him tick? Why did he do the things he did? Why marry and then virtually ignore three very attractive women? Why build a great mansion as one's health is failing? Why continue to drink heavily and use drugs when the effects obviously are so devastating?

In November 1961, two years after Flynn's death, his father wrote to Earl Conrad suggesting they meet and try to solve "the enigma of Errol." Seven years later, shortly before his own death, Professor Flynn chatted with Tony Thomas in Rosemary's Washington home and once more raised the perplexing question of "his enigmatic Errol."

As Lionel Godfrey pondered this same conundrum, he compared Flynn's demise to what happened to John Garfield and F. Scott Fitzgerald and invoked Ann Sheridan's often-repeated comment: "He was one of the wild characters of the world, but he had a strange quiet side. He camouflaged himself completely. In all the years I knew him, I never really knew what lay beneath, and I doubt if many people did."

Chapter 2 of the Tony Thomas book is entitled "The Enigmatic Errol." Thomas says he sees Flynn much like an imposing statue that "overwhelms" from afar but on close examination proves to be marred by blemishes. Nevertheless, he quickly adds, it still commands one's attention. But the truly satisfied, successful man, Thomas observes, does not wallow in booze and drugs, and his next chapter discusses at length the possibility that Flynn the actor was, in fact, a frustrated writer.

Conrad's "Memoir" opens with still more musings about Errol's enigmatic ways, his individuality, his very unique qualities. Flynn was, in a sense, he writes "an untamed brother of the sky." The rest of us, ordinary, domesticated geese, watch in awe each spring and fall as our wild, free-flying relatives wing silently overhead en route to destinations hundreds of miles away.

Although Conrad doesn't claim to have solved this riddle, in his final chapter he shrewdly observes that Flynn was much like Don Quixote, a baffling mix of fiction and fable. . .a bigger-than-life figure who threw his body at the world in an attempt to extract sensations from it Don Quixote attacked windmills and herds of sheep that, in his eyes, were giants and legions of armed might. Flynn did battle with other men, women, alcohol, drugs, stultifying conformity, and perhaps his public image as well. Conrad warns that trying to make sense of Errol is well nigh impossible since we are dealing largely with fable, his dream of what he wanted to be, not reality.

Nevertheless, Earl Conrad may be onto something here. The Man of La Mancha, "an old-fashioned gentleman" of 17th Century Spain, devoured tales of romance and chivalry, sincerely believing every word that he read. Then, fancying himself a medieval knight, he set forth alone to right wrongs and defend the oppressed, only to return home battered and bruised.

Soon, however, he acquired the services of a neighbor, Sancho Panza, who agreed to become his squire and things changed. Sancho, "a country laborer and a good honest fellow" of practical bent, brimming with basic common sense, now was at his side to remind him of the parallel existence of two worlds: the imagined and the real.

Errol Flynn, like all of us, dreamed dreams, but his were compounded by sudden success, female adulation, lots of money, and film roles that sometimes seemed to fuse with his off-screen existence. What he needed was a Sancho Panza, someone to tap him on the shoulder or crack a bottle over his head, anything to make him snap out of his all-consuming fantasies and face the real world. Lacking such, he blazed across the heavens like some new comet, dreaming as he went, and plunged to earth in his fiftieth year. . . about the age of Don Quixote was when he launched his spirited campaign to reform the world.